Prai
A Moth

"*A Mother's Grace* is filled with stories about the strength and resilience of women. Maternal energy sustains life and our planet. Michelle Moore has done an amazing job of showcasing that the givers of life are also the ultimate protectors of life. Michelle's book touched me deeply."

—**Candice Rosen**, author of
Forget Dieting! It's All About Data-Driven Fueling

"Women historically have not been able to have their stories of sacrifice and determination adequately portrayed. *A Mother's Grace* offers a poignant account that identifies the urgency of telling the stories of women who have given from the heart. Women can change the world, and *A Mother's Grace* shows us how."

—**Anandhi Narasimhan, MD**,
child, adolescent, and adult psychiatrist;
asylum evaluator, Physicians for Human Rights

"Michelle Moore describes her own physical and emotional challenges— and her resilience. Working through multiple traumas, she became stronger and found ways to offer other women what she herself needed—physical, emotional, and spiritual support. She invited twelve wounded and healing women to each write a chapter here about their journeys, and to help her create a foundation to help others, modeling for them how to 'pay good forward.' Specific guidelines are included that encourage women to learn self-reflection, define their own particular talents, create a plan to reach out to help other women and children, and even to begin their own philanthropic ventures if they choose. She urges readers to help 'heal the world' making it kinder and safer for others. The book is a gem."

—**Karen J. Clayton**, sociologist, social worker,
author of *Demystifying Hospice: Inside the Stories of Patients and Caregivers*

"With *A Mother's Grace*, Michelle Moore touches the hearts and minds of all women who have struggled through hardship, grief, and loss. Her story resonates with my own, as I lived through every parent's worst nightmare— losing a child and three bouts with lung cancer. We are not just survivors. We are a phoenix, not unlike the mythological bird that rises from the ashes to empowerment. Michelle's inspirational story illustrates our ability to morph adversity into purpose—with passion. Kudos to Ms. Moore for being a role model for all women hoping to heal from insufferable wounds."

—**Joan E. Childs, LCSW**,
psychotherapist and inspirational speaker;
author of *I Hate the Man I Love*

"Unless one experiences hardship, grave illness of a child, or even looking squarely into the face of one's own death, one misses the opportunity to empathize with others who also experience devastating need, loss of a beloved, or the annihilation of the home and village that had been the ancestral home before a tornado. Through acquaintances with strong, inspirational women, Moore found personal healing through faith, love, service, and friendship to others by sharing and writing about their experiences. By writing this poignant book, volunteering with disaster clean-up, and founding Mother's Grace, a nonprofit that now assists mothers and their children in the midst of tragic life events, this dynamic Power Woman was able to face her adversity, become resilient by grace, and raise her soul to a higher place."

—**Dr. P. D. Sargent**, author of
Power Women: Lessons from the Ancient World

A Mother's
GRACE

HEALING THE WORLD,
ONE WOMAN AT A TIME

MICHELLE MOORE

Health Communications, Inc.
Boca Raton, Florida
www.hcibooks.com

Library of Congress Cataloging-in-Publication Data
is available through the Library of Congress

ISBN-13: 978-07573-2366-9 (Paperback)
ISBN-10: 07573-2366-9 (Paperback)
ISBN-13: 978-07573-2367-6 (ePub)
ISBN-10: 07573-2367-7 (ePub)

Publisher: Health Communications, Inc.
1700 NW 2nd Avenue
Boca Raton, FL 33432-1653

Cover design by Larissa Hise Henoch
Interior design and formatting by Lawna Patterson Oldfield

To Jackson, Brooks, and Griffin,
my beautiful boys and daily inspiration.
And to my mother,
Kathleen Schwen,
the heart and soul of this book.

CONTENTS

FOREWORD

I have often thought that motherhood is the most under-celebrated profession. It took me fifty-five years to fully appreciate that I've accomplished something quite profound: mothering and nurturing three human beings. They are fine young men, who are already making a positive difference in this world through their achievements, kindness, and compassion. It isn't always easy, as any mother knows. We all experience our fair share of disappointments, setbacks, illnesses, fights . . . and there have been plenty of days when I thought I had failed. I persevered, though, because there was no choice. I am their mom; my love for them is immeasurable. This is my job, and there is no quitting, changing profession, or retiring. I cannot imagine anything more rewarding or any time that I have experienced more true grace.

In *The Bucket List*, Morgan Freeman's character Carter Chambers said, "You measure yourself by the people who measure themselves by you."

I hope that I've provided my boys with admirable standards for their own measurements. Just as I've strived to be a positive role model for my kids, I have been lucky to find an amazing role model of my own, someone who continues to show me how to be resilient through adversity by grace.

The way Michelle Moore has overcome circumstances in her own life to affirm and support other women is beyond inspiring. She is a force! If I imagined myself trying to cope with all of the obstacles she has faced, I would be paralyzed, but Michelle has not only survived an onslaught of challenges; she has thrived. I am so fortunate to call her my friend, in spite of her slippery tendency to inhabit a Type-AAA personality. I suppose that's how she gets so much done every day—at work, at home, and within the organization Mother's Grace, where I am honored to serve on the board of directors. Through my position there, I see Michelle constantly setting such a positive "can-do" tone with her attitude, which always seems to inspire our growing numbers of supporters and volunteers.

Not only am I proud to be Michelle's friend, I am especially honored to present her newest project, *A Mother's Grace: Healing the World, One Woman at a Time.*

This book is full of strong, inspirational women. You'll be moved to tears by this collection of mothers, which includes a nun in India working to overcome poverty and homelessness; a mom who's changing the face of childhood cancer; a military mom who started TAPS, a grief support system for military families; and several other remarkably inventive women. Every one of them is a living example of the power and potential of divine connections.

The women you will meet here, beginning with Michelle, will tug at your heart strings and trigger your mind, empowering you to do good things for others.

Michelle highlights the struggle and heartache that often accompanies motherhood and what mothers can accomplish when faced with overwhelming life circumstances. These moms are to be celebrated. They give us all hope that, through grace, we can endure and come through these trying times stronger and better equipped to offer struggling moms a lifeline. They offer inspiration and wisdom through their resilience and determination to help others.

Mother's Grace is unique in the immediacy of our response to families in need. In the aftermath of a crisis, we often see women barely hanging on. We offer them a lifeline, so that they are not alone in their struggle. These women are caretakers, and when we say, "We are here to help *you* because you are always helping others," they are overcome with gratitude and are provided the greatest gift of all—hope for the future. This is the work of Mother's Grace.

I am deeply committed to our mission and always moved by the nominations we receive for moms in need of support. These stories are often full of overwhelming suffering, and as a board we are grounded in gratitude for the assistance we are able to offer, inspired by our friend and leader, Michelle. Her unbridled enthusiasm is our constant inspiration. I love her dearly and treasure her friendship. May I suggest you read this book, and, when you finish, pass it on to someone you love.

—*Angela Ducey, First Lady of Arizona*

ACKNOWLEDGMENTS

I wish to thank all the strong, loving, grace-filled moms who have shared their unconditional love with me in my life: Verla, Dorothy, Sheila, Joanie, Marylee, Carol, Angela D., Sandy, Jessica, Angela R., Jodi, Manisha, Mary, Delcia, Brenda, Natalie, Romy, DeAnn, Lisa, Rina, Dawn, Hillary, Angela S., Mary Jane L. Aunt Mary, and of course our Mother Mary!

Thank you to Lara Piu and Nancy Rosenfeld, two wonderful catalysts for action, who dropped into my life out of nowhere and kicked me into high gear.

A special thank you to my writing partner and editor, David Tabatsky, who worked with me passionately and diligently to bring these pages to life. I will always hold dear the hours we holed up in Arizona, bantering back and forth for the perfect delivery. David helped me bring my vision to life, patiently prodded me for more, and made me laugh out loud many times when I really just wanted to cry. I can't wait to work with David again and suggest you all snap him up as your own writing partner.

And finally, to the grace-filled women who agreed to be part of this book. Your dedication, discipline, strength, humility and open hearts are what this world needs more of . . .

INTRODUCTION:
Finding Grace, One Mother at a Time

When Jeanette Mare's young son died without warning, she found healing through creating the Ben's Bells Project, whose volunteers make and distribute whimsical, colorful ceramic bells that inspire people to spread *intentional* kindness. Jeanette's work has received national attention, starting in 2011 when she hung more than 1,400 bells around Tucson, Arizona, in the wake of a deadly shooting at a constituent event held by U.S. Rep. Gabby Giffords. Many more bells are on the way.

Since being diagnosed with cancer in 2014, Romy Wightman has endured ten surgeries and years of treatment. Facing financial struggle, she founded a support group to share alternative options. Romy is not "cured" but, after seeing so many families face bankruptcy, she was inspired to start Wight Horse, a nonprofit devoted to helping people manage their medical debt.

After Karla Rauch's toddler, Emmett, swallowed a remote control battery and sustained permanent esophageal damage, this stay-at-home mom mobilized the Energizer company to change how button batteries are used. Driven to promote healing for other families she launched The Battery Controlled, an award-winning awareness campaign to inspire parents and physicians to control the senseless dangers of batteries and battery-controlled devices.

These three mothers, along with the ten amazing women you are about to meet, are unsung heroes and standard-bearers of grace. They sacrifice and save us. They nurture and heal us. They guide and teach us. They have followed their own intuitive path toward grace and set us on a path to forge our own future, and for most of them, it began with their children.

That's how it happened for me. As a mother of three, I can say—and mothers everywhere will likely agree—that the overwhelming love we feel when our first child is born is often mixed with apprehension, as we realize that this new life, so dependent upon us, does not come with an instruction manual, and that the world can be scary.

As a brand-new mom, I grappled with intense emotions of love and anxiety. My firstborn weighed more than 10 pounds and I was barely 120 pounds, fresh from a C-section and alone, as my family lived on the opposite coast.

"Fake it till you make it" was my mantra because I was unsure of everything at that point—*especially* whether I was equipped to be a mother. I didn't even want to leave the hospital, convinced that I would not be able to protect my son at home. At that point, I picked up a magazine and read about a couple whose son had just been killed. The father was home with the kids while the mother was out on errands. He told their fourteen-year-old son that he could take out his ATV as long as he stayed around the house. Minutes later, the father heard a terrible crash, a loud moan, and then eerie silence. For a terrifying moment, he couldn't move, unable to process the possibility of what was outside. But within seconds, he sprinted out the door and found his son convulsing, dying in front of him. As the father watched his son take his last breath, he smelled the sweet scent of chocolate chip cookies coming from his mouth. In that moment, the father was unable to comprehend how his son could be eating cookies one minute and dead the next.

Even now, twenty-two years later, this story still makes me tear up. At the time, all I could think about was how I was going to protect my son from every little thing. Over the years, I've come to realize, like most parents do, that all I can do is pray, teach, and do anything in my power to create a safer world for them and the children they will someday have.

This is why the women in this book inspire me. Everything they do may turn out to be the one thing that protects their child—and yours—from gun violence, cancer, or loss. Each of them has turned her suffering and grief into something bigger for others.

The first deep tragedy of my life occurred when I was a little girl —my mother died suddenly, out of the blue. That devastating event ignited my lifelong search to fill the hole her death created—a motherly presence, and the security and love of a close-knit family. Years later as a single, working mother, I faced life-changing challenges including cancer, divorce, and taking care of a son whose life was in grave danger from juvenile diabetes.

Throughout this time, I kept searching for a supportive community that could not only understand my situation but inspire me to find more meaning in my life, and to help me make this world a safer, healthier, and better place for our families. With the help of twelve phenomenal moms/board members, we established what became our award-winning nonprofit, Mother's Grace. The infrastructure eventually came to help thousands of families facing traumas of all kinds, and we're growing stronger and expanding every day. Our mission has become my calling, and when I set my mind to something, I don't stop. I'm a gentle bulldog: determined, relentless, and focused, except when I'm not, when I'm vulnerable like anyone else.

It's really that simple. When even one of us steps up to pay it forward, the ripple effects are awesome, and the results are long-reaching and perhaps everlasting. In fact, if you accept my invitation right now, you can find out for yourself how the true power to change lives resides within each of us.

As the "narrator" of this collection, I can say with certainty that each of the mothers in this book were divinely inspired. I've seen firsthand how they impact audiences during live presentations. Their themes include surviving natural disaster, poverty and homelessness, childhood addiction and suicide, and life-threatening illnesses. While their spiritual journeys are certainly moving, it's the actions they've taken that connect most with people. You'll find parts of yourself in these stories of seemingly average moms and be inspired to find that piece of you, which may only need a little nudge to take the next step.

One thing is certain: mothers are the backbone of our families and our communities.

This is the message I share, from community groups to large non-profits to numerous media outlets, as I form new partnerships with socially responsible corporations and philanthropic organizations. All of them celebrate women's resilience and grit.

As the founder and executive director of Mother's Grace, a non-profit organization supporting thousands of women in crisis each year, as well as in my ongoing role as a senior vice president at Laboratory Corporation of America (LabCorp), a world-leading healthcare diagnostics, S&P 500 company, I'm committed to my mission of calling attention to these selfless heroines and their causes, which now includes bringing this book before the public.

Our mission is to produce a new generation of women stepping into leadership roles. Through our mentorship programs and seed grants, Mother's Grace propels women to take the next step in supporting their communities. To date, our 100-percent volunteer-driven organization has raised more than $5 million for women and their families in need, and has assisted more than 6,000 mothers in the state of Arizona and throughout the world.

We know that millions of people all across America and around the world face similar challenges every day. That's what continues to motivate Mother's Grace missions. We're not only gaining traction in communities everywhere; we are exploding, which bodes extremely well for each of you to find a niche under our umbrella.

Welcome to what's going on in the world of female energy and power, as I offer you an alternative subtitle to this book: *Kicking Ass, One Mother at a Time.* Once you read their stories, I'm sure you'll agree that these women are remarkable change agents.

They have changed my life forever and enabled me to find fulfillment beyond my wildest dreams through their outstanding, faith-inspired responses to crises. Through them I've found new levels of friendship, faith, and grit.

Even more important, I've found grace.

#What Is Your GRACE?

SIGNS

When I was struggling through cancer, I looked everywhere for encouraging signs, praying for longevity and time to raise my children. I began to identify with the color yellow as my sign of hope. The more I opened my heart, the more I saw yellow everywhere: a yellow bouquet of flowers on a hiking trail with no other flowers to be seen; immobile in an MRI machine and hearing "Yellow" by Coldplay come on; and sitting on the patio, praying after a rough chemo treatment, when an all-yellow spider crawled up my leg. Really? A entirely yellow spider, an eight-legged angel from God, delivering a message of hope. I kept getting these signs, as if God or some spiritual force was hitting me over the head to remind me that I was going to be okay.

Here I am, twelve years later, happy and healthy, and with a family that is thriving.

A yellow sunflower, which adorns the cover of this book, symbolizes longevity, vitality, and happiness. It is light at the end of a storm!

Each of us must define what we can do as we move forward in life—what we can refine as individuals, and what we can bring to the energy of a group and the resources of a community. These collective efforts are what give us our grace.

What's yours?

1

Michelle Moore:
HEAL "THYSELF" FIRST

You must believe,
Deep inside of you,
That you were born to
Do more than survive,
Make a living and die.
You were created with a gift
Trapped inside of you;
Your job is to find that gift
And serve it to the world.

—Dr. Myles Munroe

I n October 2005, as my eight-year-old son and I descended into New Orleans in the aftermath of Hurricane Katrina to volunteer in the relief efforts, I could see the destruction for miles—households transformed into garbage, uprooted trees and rotting brush, furniture remnants, and an endless stream of random, unidentifiable personal possessions piled up everywhere.

Once we touched down, I noticed how eerily quiet it was.

I saw faces of all ages, stunned by such sudden and total loss. Children wandered aimlessly. I saw myself in that moment, as the young girl whose life had been turned upside down in an instant. Tragedy like this, which feels so utterly insurmountable at the time, can trigger such a lack of hope.

I wondered how many young girls and boys had lost a parent in Katrina and were feeling the same utter desolation and despair I once felt.

* * * *

I grew up in a salt-of-the-earth, drama-free, quintessential midwestern family, with a large extended family nearby. Every Christmas, my grandfather would dress up as Santa, trudge through the snow, and deliver presents which, according to him, "dropped out of the sleigh," especially for me and my little sister, Jessica. I felt special, loved, and secure, which enabled me to blossom into an extroverted, bossy, and curious young girl.

My dad, Richard Moore, was a constant, reliable, and present force in our home. He worked for the U.S. Department of the Interior at the Fish and Wildlife Service. He also liked to tinker around with cars and be outdoors, working with his hands.

My mother, Kathleen Schwen, was a slender, raven-haired Irish beauty. She wore black horn-rimmed glasses, which framed her poised, mischievous eyes. Her smile was confident, reflecting all she had been through at such a young age. Although she was born with a serious congenital heart defect (a hole in her heart) that should have limited her physically, it never seemed to slow her down. She finished college at an early age, married, and became a working mother—a nurse—raising me and my sister.

Our first home was in Huron, South Dakota, out in the country, where I explored and hung out with animals for hours at a time. I had a horse named Matthew, who, in the middle of a ride, had a funny habit of stopping and plunking himself down in the middle of the road. We soon moved to a "Wonder Bread" neighborhood in Madison, South Dakota, full of charming homes with screened-in front porches, straight out of a Norman Rockwell painting. Our cozy, cool basement doubled as a perfect hiding spot from the heat, a storm, or a seasonal tornado. I was allowed to walk to school alone and cruise the streets on my banana-seat bike.

My mother had always dreamed of being a nurse, but her heart condition likely would've prevented her from even attending nursing school at that time because nursing is so physically demanding. However, her family doctor—also her neighbor—was fond of her and believed in her so much that he "adjusted" her physical so that she would be accepted to nursing school.

She didn't disappoint. One night, while alone on a shift, a 300-pound patient of hers began to code. My mother, barely 100 pounds, somehow managed to get him out of bed and onto the floor and did CPR to save his life.

My mother loved her work, making a difference in people's lives, and I vividly recall her looking so well put together in her linen nursing whites, with white hose, white shoes, and a vintage 1950s nursing hat bobby-pinned to her hair. She lived her life with grace and forged ahead each day with a no-nonsense attitude, great humor, and a strong commitment to her Catholic faith.

My uncle used to tell me that his sister was "a strong, intelligent, independent, and critical thinker, in the best sense of the phrase, who did not accept any argument or persuasive message without coming to her own conclusion after careful thought. She had no difficulty expressing her opinions and you always knew where you stood with her."

She flew with pediatric heart patients being transported for life-saving surgeries. She served on right-to-life committees. She even chased down petty thieves in her bare feet one night after we had been robbed of our transistor radio. When I compare her to myself at that age, I am humbled by her accomplishments and her many quiet acts of charity and kindness.

My life suddenly changed forever on February 2, 1971. That morning, we drove downtown to buy me a pair of new patent-leather Mary Janes. My mother and I returned home with my baby sister. I skipped up the stairs to my room in my brand-new, perfect, snazzy, glamorous, stunning, stylish (did I say perfect?) shoes to get ready for school. I was ready to conquer the world, or at least my afternoon kindergarten class.

I ran downstairs to the kitchen, expecting to see my lunch set out on the big round table. But on that day, the house was quiet, and lunch was not ready. I found Jessica in the laundry room, sitting on her potty seat, and next to her I caught a sideways glimpse of my mom's feet and legs, dressed in her nursing whites, lying on the floor, pointing straight into the next room.

(Picture Dorothy's Kansas house, when it landed on the witch in *The Wizard of Oz*, as her lifeless legs pointed out from under the house . . . to this day, that image still shakes me.)

My mother appeared to be unconscious, but weird choking sounds were coming out from her throat.

"Wake up! Mommy, please wake up!"

I kept yelling as I cried and shook her.

The back-porch door slammed behind me as I ran down the street, screaming for help. Our neighbor, Mrs. Gavenboldt, heard my screams and came running frantically toward our house, looking as if it were the end of the world. It was nightfall by the time my dad returned home, escorted in a police car with flashing lights. I greeted him at the back door. A big, black hearse came and went.

I was five years old.

Our entire world fell apart. In an instant, this was the end of my family as I knew it.

"Kathy is dead!"

My father moaned in a cracked and shaky voice, as if the words were trapped in his mouth and he could only reluctantly allow them to exit. Normally strong and stable, he seemed so broken as he called my grandparents, aunts, and uncles. Family from all over arrived and filled our home that night. I was shell-shocked and kept asking why my mom had made those odd choking noises in her sleep. Later, I would discover the meaning of the "death rattle," a sound which sometimes occurs before the final breath is taken.

We laid her to rest on a cold and dark day, surrounded by somber relatives and my hysterical grandmother, who could not bear to see her daughter in an open casket, looking pasty, plastic, and grim. I was terribly frightened, too, but couldn't make sense of it all yet.

The days, weeks, months, and years that followed resembled my mom as I saw her in that casket—lifeless and hopeless. Without her, life felt empty and meaningless. My dad shut down in his own grief and later focused solely on putting our family back together.

I tried so hard to piece together memories of my mother—her bright smile lighting up a room, her infectious laugh, the poised and confident way she held herself, and the smell of her perfume. I remembered how we took a trip in a small plane and ate tuna fish sandwiches. We had so much fun. Everyone loved my mother—especially me.

Two years later, when I was seven, my dad remarried. My stepmother was the exact opposite of my mom. She was an introverted, quiet librarian who grew up on a farm and rode a horse to school. She was content to focus on her new relationship with my dad, which didn't help me feel nurtured in my immediate grief. He and my stepmother did the best they could, but back then, feelings were not prioritized, not like they are today. Like many adults of their generation, they had no idea what to do with a young child like me, dealing with such a loss.

A year later, when I was eight and still trying to get used to the new normal, life changed again. My father got a new job and with it, a transfer to Oregon, which might as well have been on the other side of the moon. My grandmother had been a second mother to me, and when we moved, I felt prematurely plucked from the womb. It was like a double death—first my mom, and then my close-knit extended family and my hometown. Any sense of stability I had quickly evaporated.

In the summers, I'd go back to the Midwest, which helped, but it was not the same as being there all the time. When I was nine, my grandmother drove me to her summer home at Lake Vermillion.

For five long hours as we drove, she and my aunt spoke on and on about my mom.

"Michelle, you're so much like her," they said. "You are physically her twin, and you act like her, too. You have the same style, and you gesture like her, with your hands moving along with your enthusiasm."

My face got hot and I couldn't breathe. I began to hyperventilate. My grandma opened the car window and told my aunt to "put her out the window" to get me some fresh air and then she pulled over so I could get my bearings. Later, I laid on her couch for days, physically and mentally ill, as if I were going crazy. My breathing was irregular, and I could swear I was dying.

This was the start of an ongoing fear, a cycle that plagued me for years. Whenever I saw someone coding on a hospital TV show, like *Emergency* with Nurse Dixie Carter, I'd have a panic attack, as I relived the death of my mother. Even when someone mentioned how much I was like her, it convinced me that I, too, might someday drop dead of a heart attack way too young.

This sequence of events triggered my relationship with anxiety and launched an endless search for a mother's comfort. I tried to bond with my stepmom and the mothers of my friends. Every time a major event occurred, one that traditionally involves a mom, I was struck with a heavy dose of melancholy. Fights with my friends, cheerleading tryouts, prom preparation, boyfriend problems, and leaving for college—all important events—left me feeling adrift and prompted bouts of illness with major anxiety, panic attacks, depression, irrational fears of dying, and loneliness. I was obsessed with trying to find the love and grace I had felt once upon a time with my mom.

By the time I got to college, my priorities were spelled B-O-Y-S and P-A-R-T-Y.

I met Rick while sitting behind him in psychology class, captivated by his broad shoulders, athletic build, and quiet strength (emphasis on the broad shoulders). He was athletic, dark, and handsome. He was sweet, but seemed a little brooding and reserved, which presented an appealing challenge. Since he was a football player and I was a cheerleader, we fell for all the bullshit things that typically influence teenagers. Hanging around with the "cool group" made me feel like I was part of a family. He liked me a lot, and put me on a pedestal sometimes, which felt great, as I had been looking for someone to care intensely about me. I was smitten and he was committed. He was also kind and loving in a way I had never experienced. I was in love with being in love. Though we were just two kids navigating a future with no idea of how to find our way, Rick was steady and had a loving family, who liked and accepted me.

On Christmas Eve, Rick got down on one knee with a pretty diamond-cut ring, which he bought himself. We married after graduating from college, moved to Atlanta, Georgia, and settled into young, exciting married life. It was the first time either of us were living far away from our families. We found our first real jobs, bought our first house, took vacations, and developed new friendships with other couples.

But eventually, truth reared its ugly head. Rick and I both struggled with emotional issues, which created a perfect storm of conflict. Whenever he was under stress, I became more anxious, controlling, and resentful.

Our "perfect" solution was having a baby, which we thought should fix everything. My first pregnancy ended in a heart-wrenching miscarriage, which just added to my debilitating anxiety over loss and abandonment. The following year, however, I gave birth to that beautiful, ten-pound baby boy, and Rick and I fell instantly in love with him.

I remember shuffling down to the nursery as soon as I could after going through a cesarean section, hunched over with stabbing pain in my stomach. As soon as I got my first peek of our son, I broke down, sobbing, gazing at our precious baby, our gift from God.

Three years later, as we navigated a move to Arizona with one young child, another on the way, and new jobs, Rick began to shut down and pull away. I rationalized that many young couples go through things like this, or maybe it was me. Maybe I was being a demanding wife by putting too much pressure on him. While I didn't know for sure, I knew that something was terribly wrong. I somehow persevered, trying my best to make everything right, and before long we had baby number three.

As our dynamic worsened, I held on tighter. Rick became more aloof, and I became scared—a perfect recipe for dysfunction. For many years, I saw a therapist and we went to couples therapy, but as hard as we tried, this dynamic continued.

In 2008, as part of what I will now declare to be my "midlife crisis," I decided to celebrate my forty-second birthday by being a slave to vanity, like some women I know, by arranging for a breast lift. While I had never considered plastic surgery, this became a present to myself, after four pregnancies and nursing three children. As part of the preparation process, the nurse inquired about my last mammogram. Though I had taken one within the last two years and had her assurance that it was fine, something in my divine inner voice told me to get another one. This was typical of my family, the "let's get this out of the way" approach.

Typically, I waited until the last minute and had the mammogram on the morning of my surgery. When I arrived at radiology,
the mammography order wasn't there, even though I was scheduled
for surgery.

"I'm having surgery today and need a mammo," I said.

Magically, and quite out of the blue, a spiritual-looking Indian
woman appeared from the back office. As her eyes peered deep into
mine, I felt a calm that slowed me down to listen.

"I heard about your story," she said. "I don't have an order, so
we can call the doctor but at this time of the morning he probably
won't answer."

I was annoyed and requested that she try harder, and she did.
Immediately following the test, a technician led me in to see the
radiologist.

"I see some calcification here that I don't like," he said, "and
although I don't think it's anything serious, I suggest that if you're
going to have surgery I would put it off for a day to make sure that
everything's okay."

Hello? Didn't he realize that you don't simply reschedule a breast
lift? I had been on the schedule for six months.

The results scared me, but I still wanted the damn surgery and
sought out a radiologist for further testing. While she didn't take
insurance, I didn't let that stop me since my motto was "let's get
this out of the way." She did the biopsy of the calcification and it
bled profusely, which first indicated a blood disorder. Unfortunately,
malignant masses bleed, too, and the next day I received a diagnosis
of cancer.

WTH?

For the next month, I endured MRIs and CAT scans and saw

more doctors than I care to remember. I was lucky because had I not gotten the mammogram and gone ahead with the surgery, I might not have survived, since I was diagnosed with an aggressive type of breast cancer, which had developed within the span of a year. I returned to thank the beautiful Indian lady for her help, but no one knew anything about such a person.

Here's the icing on that ironic cake: three weeks after my diagnosis, I had a double mastectomy, and as I was recovering from surgery, I noticed that my younger son did not look well. My typically ear-to-ear smiling boy was suddenly moody.

I wondered if he was simply worried about me. Once again, I kicked into "let's get this out of the way" mode and arranged to take him immediately to the pediatrician to check his blood sugar, which I knew to do because I work in diagnostics. Within three minutes of the urine glucose screen, we were rushed to the Phoenix Children's Hospital, where he nearly died as he hovered around ketosis and his new lifelong diagnosis of type 1 juvenile diabetes.

I was beside myself about what to do. I was about to start a year-long chemo regimen the next morning; my ten-year-old son was two hours away at a week-long basketball camp; my three-year-old was with a neighbor somewhere, bouncing off the walls; and my little seven-year-old beautiful, healthy boy was newly diagnosed with a lifelong illness that means he will have to inject a shot of insulin every time he puts something as small as a potato chip in his mouth—for the rest of his life.

Wait! What?

My brain began to shut down as they told me he nearly died and would be hospitalized for at least a week while they attempted to teach us to control his blood sugar.

I prayed for someone to wake me up from this nightmare. Pinch me, kick me, do something; just get me the hell out of here fast. I couldn't get it together and needed help, and I had nowhere to go. I called my family and my parents came immediately and everyone went into high gear to support us across the board.

The following year, I endured seventeen chemo treatments, five surgeries, and weekly appointments with five different specialists while helping my son deal with juvenile diabetes. That translated to ten pricks a day into my son's flesh, five daily shots of insulin, trying to save him from life threatening blood sugar levels and everything else that comes with such delicate territory. The ambulance was called to our home three times that first year for my son, as I was dealing with nausea, extreme fatigue, paralyzing fear, and dangerously low white blood cell counts. All the while, we were trying to save our little boy from slipping into a diabetic coma.

It was an insane balancing act. I just wanted to lie down and disappear, but I had no choice.

None!

I wanted to run away so badly and pretend that none of this was happening because it all seemed so impossible to handle. I had to suck it up and get my shit together and deal with all of it—the pain, the constant worry, the relentless physical panic, and the absolute horror that it was all on my shoulders. All of it.

I remember walking into my office and seeing months of bills and mail stacked up. I turned right around and left, unable to face it. I thought, *Why is there not a place, a person, or something to come in and ease my burden?*

That's when Mother's Grace was born.

After everything I had experienced, from age five to my current predicament, I felt the need to help other moms who were also experiencing overwhelming life crises, such as the one I had endured and was trying to currently survive. Since I had been there and lived through it, I knew I had it in me to help others.

In the meantime, my sister and best friend came over and shaved my head, which for me was more significant than having a double mastectomy. When I looked in the mirror, I saw a very sick cancer patient.

I became a mom who dragged herself out of bed, day after day, asking the same question: "Am I dying?" I had hit rock bottom, and I knew that without faith I could not deal with the relentless day-to-day trauma.

I grew disgusted with my own shit, paralyzed with fear and living in the worst parts of my head. Enough about me! I wanted to escape my own nightmare and help somebody else. I approached a couple of friends who knew my situation and my family history, and we began to raise money for mothers, like me, who basically needed a mother. I didn't think it was possible, but in our first year we raised nearly $2,000, which was used to help mothers with groceries and gift cards for gasoline and other essentials. We also drove them where they needed to go, listened to their stories, and offered encouragement.

"Hey, I'll come over and sit with you" became a familiar refrain.

"You can talk to me" was almost our motto.

I encouraged these people because I know there is grace in this endeavor we call life. I know it's hard and that it's a journey of love and light and we all need to constantly renew our appreciation for life. This comes through sitting and listening. It's not only about giving money or paying bills; we never wanted our efforts to focus solely on that.

New Orleans taught me that. We sat with moms and talked through their problems and offered help because we'd been through it and could be empathic.

For example, we helped a single working mom who needed support for her daughter with diabetes. I've been there. I got it. We helped with her mortgage and with her permission, Mother's Grace landscaped her front yard. This was the thing that made her cry. Now, she sits outside and relaxes with a glass of wine and when she arrives in the driveway at the end of the day, instead of just going into her house, she takes time to appreciate her environment.

Her reaction made me want to do more.

I had no idea what I could do or how, but that didn't stop me. As the foundation grew, I added board members with diverse expertise—an attorney, an accountant, and the First Lady of Arizona—all with different professional views who knew how to move ideas and action from point A to point B. The board of Mother's Grace now has eleven members and counting, so if one person can't help, another will step up—in the same way the women we help come to us.

Eleven years ago, when the time came for our first big fundraiser, I was mortified, afraid to show up because I feared it would be a huge flop. But seventy people showed up and donated, and it was great, not perfect but impactful. We were on our way.

Today, Mother's Grace provides mothers in need with housing costs, medication, meals, housekeeping, childcare, transportation, and more. We also work one-on-one to provide emotional support and mentorship for the long-term success of their household, and our fundraisers attract more than 500 women who raise nearly a half million dollars per event.

Now, through seed grants, we also mentor women who wish to start their own nonprofit organization. We are 100 percent volunteer-driven, and we have granted more than $3 million to women and their families in need, while assisting nearly 1,000 households per year.

Throughout my work launching and operating Mother's Grace, I struggled with cancer, chronic pain, and incessant fear. I've endured nights of back pain and neck pain, which have both kept me awake to a point where I felt that I couldn't breathe. If I had a stomach-ache, I was sure cancer was in my liver, or if I was headachy, that it had spread to my brain. It was a fricking nightmare—the constant, never-ending fear of cancer and death.

Even though two years later I was working again full-time and running a charity, the constant state of flux I was living in brought me once again into a cycle of depression and anxiety. Doctors put me on antidepressants because chemo depletes your hormones. I hated medication and fought with them until I could barely get out of bed.

Maintaining my faith was difficult as a hypochondriac. Even the example of my mother and her well-organized way of dealing with challenges was not working for me. She had trained me and my sister to respond to any emergency, which I did by seeking help when her heart failed, but this time I didn't know what to do.

Will I die and leave my children alone?

Living with cancer forced me to come to terms with my fears while empowering me to do what I had always wanted. Cancer crippled me as a person and as a parent. I wrote letters and e-mails to my doctors to ensure I would live. I prodded them with questions, and if they failed to answer, I would ask them from a different angle.

"But what if this happens; am I still going to be okay?"

Paralyzed by fear, I pleaded for a glimmer of hope.

Dr. Robert Livingston at the University of Arizona Cancer Center had a wealth of experience after many years of working with women at MD Anderson Cancer Center in Houston.

"Michelle, I really think you are going to be okay," he'd respond to my endless e-mails.

I prayed he was leveling with me, but the fear and pain was intense. Chemo was excruciating, and after one treatment, I drove to Flagstaff to focus on recovering. The physical pain was awful, but the mental games were worse. With no prognosis, I was terrified I would die. That night, I climbed into my bed and meditated deeply.

"Please, God, tell me I'm going to live."

I feared abandoning my kids, just as my mother had abruptly left me. A vivid dream came over me one night after a few desperate prayers. I recalled a buried memory as a message from my mom: that I was "the lucky one." It was my fifth birthday and I'll always remember how special my mom made me feel. I try to capture that feeling as I relate to my own children. It was the last birthday before she died, and five of my friends and I sat around the kitchen table, where we all got Charms suckers, wrapped in bright cellophane colors. As my mom handed one of those lollipops to each of us, we opened the wrappers and read the messages.

"You are the lucky one," mine read, the only one with that message.

Just like at that birthday party, when I instantly knew my mom had maneuvered for me to receive that message, I felt her once again, years and years later, responding to my prayers and offering encouragement. That was the moment, at my lowest point, when I knew I would live, when my blessed mother reminded me that I was the "lucky one" and that her presence would remain for the duration of my fight to survive cancer and help my son survive his illness.

There, by the grace of God . . .

As I discovered that day as a five-year-old, and again in New Orleans with other mothers and families, and throughout my battle with cancer, facing life head-on is doable when we discover that love is already present in our life.

We don't need to *seek* it because it *finds* us.

Our reward comes in the discovery of that truth.

＊＊＊＊

That love and the truth of my connection to it, unfolded for me in 2005 as I sat on the couch in my living room with my three sons, glued to the TV, witnessing the devastation of Hurricane Katrina in New Orleans. It became instantly clear that for thousands and thousands of families, normal life had been shattered in an instant and might never return. In the meantime, so many people needed help—physically, financially, emotionally, and spiritually. The TV was the only thing separating me from where I needed to be.

Up until then, I had never been a disaster-recovery-volunteer kind of gal. My extracurriculars involved yoga and hiking, and I never turned down a spa day, shopping trip, or relaxing vacation. But when Katrina hit, like a once-in-a-lifetime nightmare, God spoke to me. I felt an immediate calling to show up and *do* something.

I had a demanding full-time job as a vice president for an S&P 500 company. I was barely keeping my own house in order as the breadwinner and mom of a five-person household, but as we digested the scale of what was happening and how many lives were at risk, I felt a pull. I can't explain why this suburban mom felt the need to go down to NOLA to clean up houses. I had never been there and had no friends or family nearby. I just made a call and bought a ticket.

My eldest son and I persuaded his elementary school principal to allow us to hold a gift card drive so we could raise money and bring them down to New Orleans as soon as possible.

True confession: I am not down with cleaning up mold-infested homes. In fact, my official nickname is Michelle "Purell" Moore, which I was first given when coworkers witnessed me going through TSA and obsessively scrubbing down the bins with Purell wipes. I admit to being a psycho-germaphobe, but that did not stop me from packing up my son and joining a friend and her son to travel to the source of so much pain and suffering. We immediately began organizing fundraisers and raising money, with the help of Walmart, to clean up neighborhoods.

When we arrived in NOLA, our first assignment was restoring a Catholic school that had been shut down, leaving so many kids without their second home. Eventually, we cleared out the mold from the interiors of several homes and put everything out on the curb—a family's entire collection of furniture, family photographs, and heirlooms of all kinds—soggy and moldy beyond repair. We mourned for those whose family treasures lay strewn about like garbage. For many, this represented everything they owned.

Four months after the storm, most residents had fled to Texas and nearby towns, while other families lived in makeshift FEMA trailers. Firemen were still pulling dead bodies from water-soaked homes, many of which had fallen off their foundations and were destroyed, leaving entire communities to the scrap heap of history.

For most people in New Orleans, the concept of an extended family had been rewritten. To me, one who had enjoyed a loving family growing up, I ached for the children who would not get to experience that. What was to become of those little adventurers and tomboys? I was filled with profound grief and compassion for the victims as they unburdened themselves by sharing their stories. Their vulnerability was palpable. They welcomed me, a complete stranger, and accepted my offer of support as they exposed their own raw emotion.

I came alive through this authentic sense of genuine connectivity. It was what I had been searching for since the age of five—hunting for my beloved mother, looking to find a primal connection, yearning for an inclusive and mutual understanding from facing something so staggering together. This ability to reach beyond our comfort zone with love and support for those less fortunate holds great rewards, and that gift was not lost on me.

My work in New Orleans gave birth to something new. I no longer had time for bullshit excuses, drama, or gossip. Instead, my focus is on real friends who are there for each other in an authentic and accepting way.

I am equally straightforward in business and personal relationships, and diligent about not wasting time. The ability to be present, to look directly into someone's eyes and really hear what they are trying to actualize and feel, is a vital way of life for me.

Often, as I sit and listen to the feelings of others, I contemplate the best type of action for their situation. I've made it my goal to listen, to relate, to let them know they are heard, and then fly into action. In the grand scheme of life, I've learned not to be upset by stupid small stuff, such as petty drama and trivial things. Real life, real feelings, being there for another human being, and letting God lead the way is all that matters now.

This became crystal clear to me in New Orleans. I evolved as a person because of this transforming experience—metamorphosing from a Scottsdale suburbanite who knew only how to write and mail a check (philanthropy from afar) into a woman who was able to support from the bottom and directly understand the plight of others.

It wasn't always like this for me—not at all! How many kids in New Orleans were now facing the same plight and desperately needed a mother's grace and guidance? How many mothers were feeling alone, and anxiety ridden?

The moms in NOLA who were laden with loss kindled a feminine bond I had so long craved, almost as if the world dropped off as we sat, soul to soul. I listened to their stories and became part of their lives. I was there to help, but I was healing as much as they were, as I reconnected with everything I had previously associated with my mother—pain, loss, strength, and tenacity.

In New Orleans, I found a sense of belonging, a deep connection in my soul, which had been missing for so long. I discovered the true power of empathy rather than sympathy. In the midst of destruction and great loss, we cried and prayed together. Besides the obvious heartwarming experience, it was also the most fun I ever had—as a woman, mother, and fellow citizen. I found love in New Orleans and helped to create more of it.

I decided to document the stories of the remarkable women I'd met. I had no idea how I could make a difference, as a single mom trying get through life day by day. How was I going to succeed at helping others when I probably needed help keeping my own life together?

To this day, I still search for signs and comfort. As mothers, our only option is to forge ahead and so we rise each day and try again—for ourselves and for others. When I cry myself to sleep, overwhelmed by all I have experienced and feeling much of what so many others are facing right now, I grab my rosary, which makes me feel like I'm being held. That's my link to the Divine, and you may have your own—whatever works!

I breathe. I pray, and I fall asleep. The next day, I feel a renewed faith to keep doing the right thing, making the right choices, and staying on the right path. Like all of us, I get anxious and cry and sometimes err in judgment, but there's nothing complicated about how I face my challenges. It's a matter of bringing my pain to God, releasing control, and inviting grace in, especially a mother's grace. Rallying is part of my character, which I've been doing since the day I was born, and which I naturally was forced to do when my mom died.

"Michelle is bossy and a leader," my kindergarten report read, and I cannot remember a time when people failed to see me as tough and strong and able to rally, no matter what.

Like most human beings, though, I crave love and support, and, like most of the mothers in this book, we don't strive to look strong. It's a matter of survival. On lonely, painful nights, we crave someone to come in and care for us and take the pain away.

I rely on an inner voice, which often tells me to "get up and go," which I do. Perhaps this instinct was passed on to me by my mother and my grandmother, and my father, too, who shared a similar tenacity and perseverance.

"Pull up your bootstraps," my grandmother would say. Dad, a dedicated government employee, churned it out daily, and the two of them were my role models.

But I'm just Michelle, a person adverse to the label "strong" because it makes me sound tough—like I have both fists up, ready to fight. That's not who I am. Even with losing my mother and watching her die, being diagnosed with cancer, the loss of my thirty-year marriage, and my son's illness—I'm still quick to laugh—a smiling, sarcastic, and well-adjusted human being, with no magical powers other than the will to live and a strong faith.

I'm built like everyone else, and if I can rally, so can you. My fears are normal, and hopefully, I will never lose the ability to laugh at myself.

I've spoken with women from all walks of life about how our fears hold us back from doing things we know are meant to be our God-given direction. These discussions, hundreds of them over the past decade beginning in New Orleans, have struck a chord in me. For years, I was too afraid to put one foot in front of the other. By meeting so many inspirational women, I have heard the call—from within and above—to find my voice and to use my skills and drive to make concrete differences in the lives of thousands of women and their families.

As a spiritual woman, I can think of no greater calling in life. As a member of the world community, I know it's my honor and obligation to serve others, and my hope is that this book will only expand my reach and improve the lives of so many in need of love, empathy, and hope.

P.S. FROM MICHELLE

At the end of the day, if I can survive my shit, anyone can. My family, my career, my friends, and Mother's Grace have always been there for me. I only needed to step in and make it real, and I wake up each day committed to continuing that mission.

#What Is Your **GRACE**?

LONGING

I have spent forty-nine years longing for the touch of my mother. I have wanted her to hug me, hold me, wipe my tears, rub my back, and give me counsel on all matters—girl drama, work advice, marriage, and most of all, the parenting of each of my three boys.

Even now, as a responsible executive, and parent of three emerging men, I still cry out from my bed for my "mommy" whenever I get scared. In those moments, I pray that she and God are together, watching over me, along with my two grandmas, Auntie Anne, Grandpa Tom, and the whole damn crew, guiding me and keeping me safe. (It takes a village right?)

I know I was loved and cared for and most likely am guarding the most loving memories to protect myself from the pain of that loss. From a very young age, I felt a presence trying to convince me that I was going to be okay. This life force, full of energy and love, has remained with me, magically guiding me to the better side of strife, always allowing me to end up on the right side of things, guided by my angel.

Who is the angel you long for right now?

2

Connie Uddo:
SURVIVING HURRICANE
KATRINA

Strong women aren't simply born.
They are made by the storms they walk through.

—Anonymous

MEET CONNIE UDDO

New Orleans changed me forever. My transformation began when I met Connie Uddo, Executive Director of St. Paul's Homecoming Center. The Center was one of the first organizations to mobilize after Hurricane Katrina. They organized mass resources so neighborhoods could rebuild the lives they once knew and loved, and I was struck by Connie's feistiness, grand spirit, and hard work. Our group had immediately been escorted to her upon arrival in the city. They were still pulling bodies out of the water, and New Orleans was like a war zone. I knew that only a woman with a serious amount of grit could take on the kind of destruction left in the wake of Katrina.

Connie empowered our group and countless others to record the destiny of this iconic city. What most impressed me about Connie was her sincerity and deep humility. I knew our meeting was divine because as I got to know her better, I saw her as a real person, not as a superhero.

Prior to the storm, this five-foot powerhouse who was mobilizing an entire city had been a part-time, stay-at-home mom/vitamin retailer/ tennis coach. But Hurricane Katrina drove Connie and her family out of the life they knew, and when they eventually returned, she felt empty. Like many residents of New Orleans, Connie became overwhelmed with anxiety and could not drag herself out of bed.

Connie's grace, like many of the mothers you will meet in this book, came in the form of purpose. When she was called to serve, she responded and assumed the directorship of the Center to supervise her city's recovery. She nearly single-handedly developed a command central hub where residents could find resources and volunteers for the infinite challenges they faced. During that time Connie coordinated more than 9,000 volunteers and helped to restore countless shattered homes and lives.

Today Connie continues her work through the NOLA Tree Project, a tree planting nonprofit organization dedicated to growing stronger, healthier communities through tree planting and community service projects. The organization has, to date, replanted and given away more than 55,000 trees. Connie has also won numerous awards, served on several boards and committees, testified at a U.S. Senate Hearing, was featured on NBC Nightly News with Brian Williams, and was a featured guest on ABC's Secret Millionaire where she was awarded $40,000 for her work. Now Connie's in great demand, as she inspires groups of all sizes *including corporations and organizations around the country.*

Once a woman with depression who could barely run her house, Connie's inward restoration began when she let go of fear and let grace in. As she helped heal her city, the city healed her. My experience in New Orleans taught me that we are united in emotion, empathy, grace, and divinity. Hurricane Katrina forever transformed everyone involved in the tragedy, and Connie's story will forever change you.

Connie Uddo responded to the devastating loss created by Hurricane Katrina by placing herself on the front lines of her community's recovery. Initially depressed as a result of the utter devastation she saw and felt all around her, Connie discovered grace and, as a result, founded St. Paul's Homecoming Center, a Hurricane Katrina recovery hub, which provided resources, volunteer coordination, and case managers for more than 60,00 homes devastated by this climate catastrophe.

In this chapter, she explains how the experience improved her own life and transformed her family and her community at-large into better people, now equipped with a new level of empathy and a passion for providing concrete assistance to those in great need. Connie, who has been featured on CBS Sunday Morning and a PBS ten-year anniversary documentary, along with countless other media outlets, shares the exact approach she used to get through the storm and pay it forward.

Meet my dear friend, Connie Uddo, in her own words.

S treamers, balloons, and the aromas of dinner filled our house as we celebrated my daughter's "Sweet Sixteen." It was a memorable night to share with friends and family, that is, until one of our friends hit me with an unexpected question when she arrived to pick up her daughter.

"Why aren't you getting ready for the storm?"

"Well, it's way out in the Gulf. It's not even a Cat 3 yet," I said.

At that point, I felt quite casual about the approaching hurricane.

"You better get ready," she said.

"No, we'll be fine."

As a New Orleans native, Hurricane Katrina didn't alarm me. I had survived many wicked storms and never had to evacuate, especially for a Cat 3. My husband, Mark, and I had done the usual: boarded up windows and stocked up on batteries, flashlights, and water. We had also filled our bathtubs with water, but we weren't sweating any impending catastrophe.

Funny how category *and* catastrophe *both begin with the same three letters.*

I was a tennis instructor with a vitamin sales side hustle (a side job), and my husband was executive chef at a local private school. In anticipation of the kitchen coolers going down, his employer sent food home with him. Since our house sits up high, we invited friends, family, and neighbors to come on over and ride out the storm.

The next morning, I woke up at five o'clock, thank God, because by then Katrina had escalated to a Category 5 and our area of town had been placed under mandatory evacuation.

"Everybody get out. You need to evacuate now!"

The mayor was issuing warnings on every local television network.

"If you don't get out, you better have an ax to remove yourself from your attic. If you stay, you're in terrible trouble because this is a big storm and could hang New Orleans."

We all went straight into panic mode and scrambled to pack.

"My mom is on a breathing machine," my cousin said. "You've got to get her out."

I decided to drive her to Houston in our car caravan as soon as we could get on the road. All hell broke loose as noon approached when my mother-in-law refused to leave.

"I've been through the Depression," she said. "I've been through the war. I've been through a hundred hurricanes. I'm not leaving." She was adamant and prepared to stay.

"You all are crazy for leaving," she said, rolling her eyes at all of us.

This scared me to death, but we had to go so I ended up leaving my husband with his mother. Just before our departure, our family held hands and prayed in our driveway.

"I hope I see you again," I told Mark.

We headed off into a great unknown.

It's typically a six-hour drive from New Orleans to Houston, but our trip took fourteen grueling hours. The freeways became parking lots, filled as if the entire city was trying to escape. The whole scene looked like one of those end-of-the-world movies where a giant asteroid is coming to wipe everyone out. Finally, at four o'clock the next morning, we arrived in Houston.

Back in New Orleans, the storm pounded the city with relentless force. Unable to sleep, I watched the nightmare play out on television. In this case, I knew the devastation was real and that I wasn't watching a movie of the week.

For the next three days, I repeatedly called my husband, but I couldn't get through as all the phones were dead. This put me in a panic, but on the outside, I tried to keep it together for our kids. I finally got through to Mark and discovered they were okay. My mother-in-law was located in the 20 percent of the city that did not flood. In fact, they were unaware at first that the city was flooding at all. When the storm passed and they turned off the radio to begin cleaning up, a neighbor saw them in the yard and called out to them.

"Hey, do you know what's going on?" he said. "You need to get out of the city. It's mayhem. All hell is breaking loose."

My husband turned the radio back on only to discover that the levees had broken, there was rampant looting, and martial law was in effect. New Orleans had turned into Armageddon.

"Look, Mom," he said. "I love and I respect you, and I know you don't want to, but we are leaving, and we are leaving now!"

When the storm finally passed, the Seventh Street Canal breach flooded our middle-class neighborhood for a month, causing catastrophic damage. It seemed forever before we were finally allowed back to check on our house. We were considered one of the "lucky" ones because we actually had something to work with when it came to our house. The first floor was completely lost, but the other two floors were okay.

Otherwise, we were in shock. The city itself seemed like a ghost town. We found bodies being pulled from homes and looters making their way through various neighborhoods. For a month, ten to twelve feet of water sat inside people's homes, creating devastating mold and structural damage. Nothing was salvageable. Neighborhood schools had been destroyed or shuttered. Overwhelmed by the daunting task of rebuilding, a large percentage of New Orleans residents didn't return to the city they knew and loved. I'd run into people and ask them what they were going to do.

"Are you going to stay and rebuild?"

They looked at me, bewildered, as if doomsday had hit, which it certainly had.

"I just don't know."

I heard this refrain repeated over and over, as people tried to absorb the magnitude of what had happened to their lives. Some folks with flood insurance were covered, but most were not. Others had insurance but could barely scrape up enough money to cover all the roof damage. After the U.S. Army Corps of Engineers admitted that the levees had been improperly built, which meant the disaster was man-made, the federal government created what they called the Louisiana "Road Home" Program. It was meant to provide funding to rebuild houses damaged from the levees, but unfortunately the program was poorly run. There was not enough funding, and the money that was granted was impossible to access. Everywhere people turned, they ran into a ton of red tape, with no funding for wind damage, either. Foreclosures eventually forced thousands and thousands of residents to leave New Orleans permanently.

We relocated six times in a four-month period and our kids attended three different schools. I don't think they learned anything much academically during that entire school year, but they certainly learned a lot about life and how unfair life can be, and that water doesn't discriminate. It devastated everyone—rich and poor. No one was spared. Five months after the storm, our house had electricity again and everyone in the family but me wanted to return.

"We are so tired of living out of boxes and sleeping on air mattresses," my kids said. They never wanted to complain, but their concerns were valid.

"We want to be in our own beds. We don't care anymore if anybody is there. We want to go home."

Despite the lack of stores, streetlights, and mail delivery, not to mention safety, I decided to give it a try. We were among the first ten Lakeview residents to return out of the 8,000 residents whose homes had been devastated, along with ruined businesses, churches, and schools. Our entire neighborhood looked like the aftermath of a nuclear bomb.

We felt like western pioneers discovering a new town. Looting remained a problem, as amateur criminals from all over the country would walk into homes with intact second floors and help themselves to anything and everything that was portable: television sets, jewelry, cash, and computers. Local police departments fell apart amidst the endless challenges, and while the National Guard was present, its coverage was sporadic.

When my car was robbed, that was the last straw for me. I went over the edge.

"I can't do it. I can't live here. This is not living."

I was severely depressed and had hit rock bottom by that point.

"Look, honey," Mark said, "we've moved six times. Do you really have the energy to move again? We have a roof over our heads, and I have a job. The kids are back in school. We've gotten ahead of this whole thing. When you realize that people have lost everything —their jobs and businesses and homes—you have to see that in a way we're ahead of the game. Maybe you just need to find a new purpose here because where are we going to go? We can't sell our house. It has no value and all of our equity is locked up in our home."

Mark had a job, but not me. With the tennis courts where I had been teaching underwater, and my students gone, I was lost. I cried and cried and could scarcely drag myself out of bed, but Mark was right. In his gentle, wise way, he had it just right.

I had to find a way to regenerate my life.

I took a brief retreat in the attempt to pull myself together. Facedown, I prayed to God from my devotional and asked for guidance. "Please show me what to do and how to do it."

On the following day, I discovered my answer in my Bible on page two of Chronicles 32: 7–8:

BE STRONG AND COURAGEOUS; DO NOT BE AFRAID
OR DISCOURAGED BY YOUR ADVERSITY, FOR THERE IS A
GREATER POWER WITHIN YOU THAN THE ADVERSITY.
WITHIN YOU IS THE LORD OUR GOD TO HELP YOU
AND TO FIGHT YOUR BATTLES.

I read the passage three times and instantly knew this was my answer. I didn't even have to work very hard at all to convince myself.

You don't want me to run away. You're telling me to face it, and I'm here, and if you include me on this and I'm here and you come to me—I am with you. Don't be afraid. Face it. Don't run away.

I began to come around. I pleaded for help.

Show me how to stay. I'm in. I surrender. Show me how to stay. Show me how to survive.

When I returned home, I shared my new perspective with Mark.

"I'm thinking that the government is providing trailers," I said, referring to the FEMA trailers provided for people to park in front of their homes as they rebuilt. "I see some trailers coming into the neighborhood, so why don't we try to have a meeting with some other families at our house? We can talk about how to protect ourselves, what our needs are, and what is needed to rebuild, together."

"Great idea!" said Mark.

I made a flyer, and my kids and I got on our bikes and rode through our little neighborhood. Everywhere we saw a car or a trailer or some evidence of life, we placed the flyer in someone's hands and told them our plan. "Hey, we're having gumbo and wine at the house for a neighborhood meeting."

When that night came, I looked out the window and was shocked that people were actually coming. It felt as if the catacombs were opening since everyone had previously been so unsocial and hunkered down with work. Even Senator Mary Landrieu, who happened to be in the neighborhood at the time, attended.

The meeting was such a hit that one day the captain of the Third District Police Department knocked on my door.

"I heard about your meeting and want to congratulate you," he said. "You are the first in the neighborhood to do anything like this, and I want you to meet someone doing the same thing in another flooded neighborhood who is a few steps ahead of you. I think you need to connect."

Denise Thornton had founded an organization from her home called Beacon of Hope. Her husband was manager of the Super Dome, where the Saints played football, among other things, and they were back in their house because he was working to rebuild the Dome. They, too, were living on their upper floors, and she, like me, had needed to find purpose in her devastated, abandoned neighborhood, when she landed on the idea of galvanizing a recovery.

"Why don't we make your house a Beacon of Hope for your neighborhood?" she said, laying out a proposal at our first meeting.

I agreed to discuss it with Mark, who didn't quite see it the same way.

"What are you talking about?" he said. "You're crazy, you know that?"

He grabbed the phone and called my sister.

"Your sister is having a nervous breakdown," he said, "crying all the time, and she can hardly get out of bed. Now, from whatever you told her, she wants to stand on the corner with a street sign that says 'Welcome! I'm going to help you rebuild.'"

My sister didn't have to answer because I did.

"Well," I said, "you said, find a purpose. I met a woman who is starting to make a little headway and here's the scripture I get."

I began to read from the Bible, when he finally gave in.

"Okay, okay," he said, "does this mean you'll stop crying and get out of bed?"

"Yes. I think it could help."

"Okay, I'm in, but it's your baby."

I understood him totally. That spring, I founded the Lakeview Beacon of Hope out of our house. I had never run a volunteer group and had absolutely no idea what to do, but I had learned about a group of volunteers living in a park nearby. They had flown in from all over the country offering their help, so I recruited them, and they came to my house every day.

"I love what you're doing," a stranger asked me one day. "What do you need?"

"I need tools. Everything is rusted and flooded. I need shovels. I need loppers. I need weed eaters. I need garbage bags. We need so much of everything just to clean the debris."

"Here's $1,000," he said, handing me a check.

God had my back.

Tools in hand, I started to bring in more volunteers to clean up entire blocks without asking for permission. If someone drove up to their house and saw that the front had been cleared of debris, dead vegetation gone and floating roof shingles and rubble put in the trash, then perhaps the situation would be less overwhelming and we could talk them into rebuilding and staying put in the neighborhood.

For four months, I ran everything from my house until St. Paul's Episcopal Church and School suggested we join forces. The neighborhood rector had succumbed to a breakdown and left, so they brought in a Navy chaplain, a captain by the name of Will Hood. At first, his task was to gather the parishioners to let them know that the parish was shuttering its doors for good. Their response took him by surprise.

"You cannot get back on your motorcycle and go to Houston because we're not closing. We don't care, and we will find a way. If need be, we'll do it ourselves."

"All right, wait a second," Hood said. "I'm a military guy. I can get down and dirty, but I'm telling you that you're going to have to do this yourself."

They promised to do whatever it took. Everyone felt duty bound and committed. Will called Bishop Charles Jenkins at the Episcopal Diocese of Louisiana and explained what had transpired.

"I can't close the church," he said. "I don't have the heart to walk out on these people. We need to give it a try, and I've decided to stay."

Bishop Jenkins approved but could not provide any financial support. That's when Will approached me about Beacon of Hope and asked if I would be willing to move the organization out of my house and into his church.

"Connie," said Will, "I can only tell you that I've been in a lot of war zones but have never seen devastation like this."

"Even in Iraq?"

"In Iraq, we had access to water and a phone line. This is much worse."

So that's when the St. Paul's Homecoming Center began.

"This is how you'll build it, Connie," said Will. "As the need comes in, you find the resources and start putting A and B together—needs and resource, needs and resource."

Leveraging that model, we expanded into a full-blown recovery center. We offered case management, which was especially needed by the elderly to learn how to fill in the required paperwork for the Road Home Program. We created a "washateria," a laundromat, in a double-wide trailer because people needed to wash their clothes. We started a tool-lending library where residents could borrow a lawn mower, gutting tools, or whatever they needed to repair their homes. Repurposing thirty Army cots that Will found, we created a place for volunteers to eat and sleep and shower, as they were coming in from all over the world, from all walks of life, to help in the recovery. It would take years before federal funding would be available to many residents, which would have made it impossible for them to even consider rebuilding. How were they supposed to pay contractors without money?

None of this happened by magic.

St. Paul's provided critical resources to hold people over until the Road Home checks arrived, and volunteers like Michelle Moore and her sons flew in from around the nation to help shoulder the rebuilding of our city. Yet, it wasn't right. Millions of dollars had been granted by the federal government, but where was it? How could we live without a post office or a grocery store or a school? Some homeowners opted to sell their homes back to the state, and neighbors feared what would become of their properties. All of this resulted in a whopping 60 percent of people who did nothing, even though help was available.

Something was desperately wrong.

Widespread depression, hopelessness, and despair took over Lakeview. At St. Paul's, I was the cheerleader who kept telling people to hang in there because we'd become a community again, but it got so bad that I could no longer look them in the eye. The future seemed bleak.

In 2007, two years after Katrina, I was invited to testify at a U.S. Senate hearing to investigate Road Home, a hybrid public/private program with more loopholes than accountability. After detailing the lack of funding, endless red tape, and the unconscionable waiting for approved funds that citizens were encountering, I ended with a story about a volunteer.

"We met a little girl from Boston who was nine years old when she arrived in New Orleans with her mother to do whatever they could to help us. On the third day of working in Lakeview, she stopped her mother in her tracks. 'When are we going back to America?' she asked. I am here to ask the same question of your subcommittee members and senators and our entire government: When will we come back to America? We want to rejoin our country. We are real Americans living in real American neighborhoods, and we want to be real Americans again. But it is just not happening, and I am here to ask you why."

After the Senate hearing, a civil action was issued but not much changed. People continued to experience many of the same problems as before, and when the Road Home contract was transferred to another private firm, we ran into the same exact issues.

In 2009, Will Hood was called back to the Navy.

"What do you want to do?" he said.

"Let's take a ride," I said.

As we drove to Gentilly, a neighborhood with 30,000 flooded homes, it looked like Lakeview once did—no center, no leadership, and total struggling.

"Man, this is bad," said Will. "This is how we looked two years ago." I nodded.

"You want to do it all over again here, don't you?" he said.

I nodded again, with a strong and clear "Yes." I've been taking on national and global disasters ever since. Our long road to recovery after Hurricane Katrina inspired one of the most treasured times in my life—right up there with the birth of my children—and I had no intention of stopping, not then and not now.

"How are you still standing?" people frequently ask, knowing I'm one of the few original people who continue to work on our city's recovery.

The answer is quite simple. I am still standing because the work keeps my life in check. Hurricane Katrina was the impetus for my unbelievable and completely unexpected life transformation, and I wouldn't have it any other way.

From start to finish, the experience has made me a better person. Before Katrina, I was focused on money and all it could buy. I wanted to take my kids all over the world and would encourage my husband to make enough money so we could afford all of it. But after Katrina, I began to change, internally and dramatically. God did such a job on me, so much so that I would never go back. While I would not wish this disaster on anyone, it has had its silver linings.

I witness miracles every day and see God's work in amazing ways. I have come to realize what is important in life, and to this day it's what keeps me in check. For me, it is my faith, family, health, and a roof over our heads.

> "FOR I KNOW THE PLANS I HAVE FOR YOU,"
> DECLARES THE LORD, "PLANS TO PROSPER YOU AND NOT TO
> HARM YOU; PLANS TO GIVE YOU HOPE AND A FUTURE."
> (JEREMIAH 29:11)

I repeat this to myself whenever I find myself whining. Hurricane Katrina transformed me and my children into stronger and better people, and money and having "stuff" does not matter anymore. Katrina cleaned us up on the inside in so many ways, and I have often relied on my children for help in this regard.

For example, one Saturday morning I had 500 trees to plant and woke my kids early to help because my volunteers had not come through.

"No!" my kids said, protesting in unison. "We're so sick of you and Katrina and we don't want to hear about it anymore. We just want to feel normal like the rest of our friends, but you're constantly making us do this stuff."

"Too bad. Sorry. I need you."

That was that. No arguments. When the day was over, I suggested they sit down so I could tell them something, and then I asked for their forgiveness. I could see they were anticipating an apology.

"I've been raising you wrong. What I'm realizing through this process is that I've been treating you like my generation, where we give you everything you want to make life as easy and cushy as possible. But that's wrong, and you know what? We really are supposed to be the givers of the world—not the other way around. I'm just realizing this now, that the work we've been doing as 'givers to the world' will eventually become our greatest joy. This, my dear children, is what life is all about—the joy of giving and of finding fulfillment."

I paused before continuing to make sure they were listening.

"From now on, we're going to give generously, and I won't kill myself to make life perfect for you because it's not going to serve you as you prepare for the real world. Life has good times and bad times and you need to know how to handle both."

For several minutes, nobody spoke. They were shocked, but they got what I was saying and never complained again.

"What do you need, Mom?" said my daughter, Stephanie, who was in high school and worked in our laundromat. Every Saturday, she and her friend would wash and fold clothing for residents so they could focus on home repairs.

My son went to Colorado State and got involved in the campus ministry. After he graduated, he did an eleven-month, eleven-country mission trip. My kids had listened, and heard, and had become inspired, not by me, but by their own capacity for giving.

"You know, Mom," said Stephanie, "I'm really thinking of becoming a nurse."

"Why?" I said.

"Two reasons. I'm good at science. But you know, after living through Katrina and doing all we've done, I need a career that helps people."

As you can imagine, I burst into tears and thanked God for using the disaster to change the hearts of my family. These were the real fruits of my labor.

Helping in the recovery of Hurricane Katrina spurred the most remarkable growth of my life. From a state of depression and feeling ten feet underground, I soared to feeling ten feet above the ground by the time our volunteers left at the end of each day. There was no time to worry about myself or my future, or our kids, or my whatever. I was totally focused and consumed with work. It was powerful, and I felt empowered. Within the span of one month, I went from being the pitiful victim to a "We can do this!" kind of woman.

Today, this experience is what has paved the way for a new and richer perspective. On the occasion I feel self-centered or impatient, I catch myself and reboot my direction.

Hurricane Katrina was responsible for transforming our community and knitting it closely together. Five years after the hurricane, Lakeview finally got a Starbucks, which became our Taj Mahal. I was in line one day when the lady in front of me gave the barista quite a hard time over her latte order.

"Excuse me," I said, tapping her on the shoulder. "Do you live in this neighborhood?"

"We just moved in," she said.

I could feel a chill in her response.

"Well, you know what, we didn't even have a coffee shop in this neighborhood until five years ago, so you need to be grateful that you even have a cup of coffee, and a coffee shop, and that begins with being nice to this woman right here."

The woman had no response. When the customers behind me began to clap, I felt fortified to offer a final comment.

"So take your stupid, imperfect latte and please go to another neighborhood where you can get the perfect cup because we're grateful for anything we have right here."

With that, I was finished.

Katrina taught me how sometimes we humans are better on our knees. The hurricane tore our city to shreds, but it also pulled us together. I witnessed New Orleans rise from the ashes as total strangers came together.

I also benefited from a more meaningful career because of Hurricane Katrina. On the tenth anniversary, as the city continued to rebuild, things were beginning to wrap up while government funding was running dry. However, the community's needs remained, and especially within the elderly population, so I transformed the Gentilly Center into a senior community center.

Five years ago, a friend with a tree planting organization, called Hike for KaTREEna, was burned out. She had planted 8,000 trees in eight years, and she also had a full-time job.

"I'm going to shut down," she told me. "I'm exhausted."

"Monique, you're so vital to the recovery. Our city lost 100,000 trees and your organization has had such a significant impact on our recovery. If you close down, what's going to happen to the tree canopy?"

She couldn't continue, so I folded her nonprofit into mine and changed our name to the NOLA Tree Project. I also added a disaster-recovery community outreach program. After Hurricane Harvey, our response was immediate, offering tools and disaster recovery know-how.

One day, there was a knock at my door and a man handed me a special envelope.

"This is from the White House," he said.

Inside, I found the President's Volunteer Service Award, signed by Barack Obama. This was exciting for a moment, but while it's nice to be acknowledged, that's not why we do what we do. You see, we all have Katrinas in our lives. Whether it's a natural disaster or an illness, the death of a loved one or a broken relationship, at some point in life we're all touched by heartache. That's when everyone needs to dig in and help.

The lesson we learned is that you're supposed to come out a better person.

Why did people come home after Katrina? Because they loved their homes, their city, and their respective neighborhoods. People wanted nothing more than to be able to cook a pot of red beans. It is this love of home and community that moves us to dig in and do what's necessary. After Katrina it was a real love fest in New Orleans as people struggled together to rebuild their beloved city. *Fleur de lis* hung on every door, and strangers came by the millions, offering help and support. This is what love looks like.

On days when I thought, *I cannot do this, I'm so tired, I'm so overwhelmed, I have no clue what I'm doing,* that love propelled me onward and became the engine of our recovery.

There's a great scripture that goes something like this:

I DON'T BRING YOU THROUGH THE FIRE
TO COME OUT CHARRED AND SCARRED, AND BURNED,
BUT CROWNED WITH THE OIL OF GLADNESS AND
JOY, AND ALL TO THE GLORY OF ME.
(ISAIAH 61:3)

We don't go through the fire to come out as victims. We are transformed by tragedy, which only makes us stronger, wiser, and the polar opposite of downtrodden.

My competitive nature kicked in and mobilized me after Hurricane Katrina. I had been a competitive tennis player, a member of the Louisiana State University women's tennis team, and after college I participated on the women's pro circuit. Katrina became the match of my life and the struggle in its aftermath required my entire being to pull myself up and do everything possible to keep my city from going down the drain, especially when so many people were arguing about abandoning the city in the wake of its destruction. No one wanted to waste taxpayer dollars to rebuild a city situated below sea level, a city riddled with poverty, which was 60 percent black.

It made me angry to see how people would give up on such a great American city with so much cultural wealth and history, an argument that only fired me up to prove our worthiness.

My competitive nature alone would never have spurred me on. It was my faith in God, which gave me the confidence to face my situation, armed with the knowledge that I would not be going it alone. It was no accident that I was placed smack in the middle of this destroyed city. I did what I could on my own, but I relied on God for the supernatural strength and shove, which all of us needed, because Katrina was much bigger than we were.

To this day, being grounded in my faith remains my key.

As they say, you don't have a testimony unless you're tested, and what a powerful testimony it can be if you get through the test with the knowledge learned, and then push each day from a greater perspective. For me, I often struggled, and shared my doubts with Will. "I should not have done this. I'm in over my head. Who am I to think stupid little me can help people rebuild their lives?"

"Look at your boots, Connie," he said one day. "Is that blood on your boot? Let me tell you, I have held dying soldiers in choppers while serving in Iraq. I do get overwhelmed like you, but I have never rebuilt a church or a school. I'm a freaking military guy, but I look at my boots and remind myself that there's no blood on them so I can do this, and that means you can do this, too. You know, there are far greater things we could be dealing with right now."

He had my attention.

"I am going to pray into you," said Will. "I am praying anointment. I am praying for grace, and for courage, and for the strength that you're going to come out of this as one of the most powerful of God's people on the planet."

This entire experience was and is to this day God-led. God has put me down the right path hundreds of times in my work. With that in mind, I have no doubt that Michelle Moore and I did not meet by accident. I just knew in my spirit when I met her and her son that she was special, and we were going to stay connected for a lifetime. Her compassion and heart to help were genuine and sincere, right from the start.

Little did I know I would be invited to speak at her first Mother's Grace event, which was an honor. At first, I didn't know Mother's Grace was just getting started, so when I found out it was the opening event, I felt a bit nervous because I wanted it to be a huge success. I had not spoken in front of large groups of people before, so I felt a bit lost up there, but the ladies were kind and gracious. Many women came up to me and thanked me for sharing my experience. It's hard to find words to describe what that day meant to me, and I could only sum up my experience to Michelle by saying, "My cup runneth over!"

Many thoughts run through my mind today as I reflect on my experience with Mother's Grace. I'm still so inspired by how Michelle put her initial fears aside and plunged ahead with her idea and dreams.

I can promise her this, that she will never look back. From my experience, once you see and feel the results of your love and labor, you're all in. The journey simply continues, taking you to many places, challenging you physically, mentally, and spiritually, but once you dig in, there's really no looking back. You feel yourself deepening and awakening as you see so many miracles emanating out of your work.

It's so much bigger than any one of us.

"NOT BY MIGHT OR POWER,

BUT BY MY SPIRIT," SAYS THE LORD.

(ZECHARIAH 4:6)

This is a scripture I live by in my work. Passing this on to my children means a great deal to me, as I know it does for all of the mothers doing God's work throughout the world. As we set the right examples, we remind the next generation of the freedom they will experience in taking "the focus off of self" by feeling the joy of giving and gaining a deeper understanding of what Christ meant when he said, "It is better to give than receive." The fruit of doing this will be their greatest reward, as they discover that there is a true champion inside them, as there is in all of us, with the capacity to ripple outward and touch thousands of lives in unimaginable ways.

I have learned from my Katrina recovery work that faith is active and powerful. It doesn't sit in a pew inside a church. It moves, and mothers and others are movers for sure!

In the end, there are no accidents or coincidences with God. When you tune into the journey, He allows you to be led by the Holy Spirit. You will sense this and begin to understand how God ordains the people you encounter, and the circumstances you end up in. All you need is an open heart and a willingness to accept blood on your boots.

P.S. FROM MICHELLE

I returned to New Orleans five years later, this time for Jazz Fest with my best gals, a trip that would not be complete without hooking up with Connie. After many hugs and tears, we caught up on all her blessed activities. Now an expert in her field, I marveled at what she had accomplished since we met. I will always be grateful for our divine meeting and the grace behind our friendship. I have great faith in the power of her story—that it will inspire other women to rise to the occasion in the face of natural disaster.

Connie may seem like she is equipped with some special powers, but she is just like you and me. She is not a saint or a world leader. She is just a normal mom, residing in a community hit by tragedy, only she chose to *do* something about it, to create exponential impact for others while raising her soul to a higher place.

Connie came back in 2010 to be our first speaker at our Mother's Grace event. What she did as a human being and a mom is what I have seen many other women do when they start from scratch, armed with an idea, a passion to make a difference, and a huge open heart, taking a thousand dollars to start an organization in their living rooms and growing it into amazing stories of transforming the lives of others.

Connie's letter to me, shared in part here, beautifully sums up our shared mission.

Michelle, my heart is still full from your beautiful event. "My cup runneth over!"

I didn't know quite what to expect and I was honored and humbled to be invited to speak and to be selected as a recipient of a Mother's Grace grant. Congratulations for putting your fears aside and going forward with your idea and dreams. I can promise you this, that you will never look back. You have begun a journey that will physically take you to many places, mentally challenge you and spiritually deepen you and awaken you as you will see many miracles from your work, which is so much bigger than us. "Not by might or power, but by my spirit," is a scripture I have lived by and I know that Mother's Grace will impact and define its own mission statement through your children. They will learn so much from watching and working with you. They will experience a great freedom in "the focus off of self" and will also experience the joy of giving. The fruit of this will be your greatest reward and they will discover the champion inside of themselves, as in all of us. Your work will ripple and touch thousands of lives in ways you can't imagine. Congratulations on putting *hands and feet* to your *dreams and faith*. I have learned from the Katrina recovery that faith is active and powerful. It doesn't sit in a pew or a church. It moves and you all are movers, that's for sure! Thank you once again for a day I will never forget.

Thanks to Connie for inspiring me to do what I do. She is a blessing for all of us.

#What Is Your **GRACE?**

BREATHE

I am impatient by nature. I must constantly remind myself to slow down, connect with the moment, and *breathe*—deep and full and open to experience true grace. This is a challenge, but I try.

About ten years ago, as another hectic school year began, I was working again, driving my kids all over town, and always thinking about my next project. I felt myself winding up into that familiar but risky hurry mode when I am often just a small step away from losing myself.

I dropped off my boys at school as usual and drove away quickly. As I prepared to turn into a large intersection, I saw a crossing guard raise her hand aggressively, as if she were talking directly to jacked up, Type-A super moms, like me. She scowled at me, ordering me to slow down and pay attention!

At first, I was annoyed, as if Little Miss Crossing Guard, with her flag and neon vest, thought her agenda was more important than mine. But then I watched this woman walk back to the curb and gently hover over a little boy on a scooter and escort him across this busy street, as if her job was the most important thing she would ever do in her life. She glared at the cars that reluctantly stopped, and the confidence she displayed in her role in that moment was powerful and moving. I was flooded with emotion and had to pull over into the Safeway parking lot where I sat in my car and just wept, trying to catch my breath.

The love and strength this woman showed was the essence of a mother's grace. In her own way, she makes the world a better place, one child and one self-important driver at a time.

What makes you lose your breath?

3

Lori Alhadeff:
MAKING SCHOOLS SAFE

And for all of the things
Changing around her,
She has found her home
In the arms of grace.
Eternally rooted
In love that sustains her,
No amount of darkness
Can tear her away.

—Morgan Harper Nichols

MEET LORI ALHADEFF

It was 1999; my firstborn was two years old and I was enjoying every
minute of motherhood. On April 20, I was at a Gymboree playdate with
my son when I got a call from my husband to turn on the news. We all sat

around the TV, watching as the Columbine massacre unfolded in front of us. It was the first time I had experienced such grief through the television and, as a new mother, it was multiplied. The next time would be 9/11 when my second child had just turned one. There is something about witnessing a human catastrophe from the safety of your living room while others, just one state away, are running around, searching for children who may have been shot in school. I still can't wrap my head around it, even after all the shootings we've seen since Columbine.

I am positive that it's every mom's worst nightmare to get a call from their child's school that there has been a shooting, or even worse, to find out your child has been involved. Columbine, Sandy Hook, Parkland. The list goes on, and the names blur. Whenever an alert pops up on my computer or my phone, describing yet another episode of gun violence, I get this sickening pit in my stomach and I try to control my emotions by making sense of it, but I simply can't. Then I veer into this place of trying to rationalize it or strategize a plan. Do I buy my son a bulletproof backpack? Can anything be done? When you feel as if nothing is possible, that the problem is just too big, then let me tell you about people, like Lori Alhadeff, who show us all that there are things to be done to make our schools safer for our children.

I am beyond humbled to introduce Lori Alhadeff in her own words.

I was a health and physical education teacher for five years after graduating from The College of New Jersey. My husband is a doctor, practicing internal medicine. My baby girl, Alyssa, was born in 2003, Robbie arrived eighteen months later, and Coby was born a few years after that. We were a bustling family and I fell into my beloved role as a traditional stay-at-home mom, taking care of our kids, cooking, cleaning, and chauffeuring the children around to their various activities. We moved to Parkland, Florida, six years ago because their schools were A-rated and considered "safe." That word would become my mantra while living in what was supposed to be a beautiful area to raise children.

In 2018, the kids were attending elementary, middle, and high school. After packing their lunches and getting them to the school bus, my personal time kicked in, and, like many middle-aged moms, I enjoyed the chance to breathe. As a lifelong athlete, I enjoyed the competitive energy and camaraderie of being on a tennis team, which meant daily practice or matches. After a few hours of fun, it was time for errands before returning home to make dinner, welcome the kids back from school, and help with their homework. Alyssa, Coby, and Robbie played soccer, and I was the classic soccer mom, driving them all over South Florida it seemed, to one practice after another, which never seemed to be scheduled at the same time or in a neighboring location. It seemed like I was constantly on the go, but that was my life and I loved it. We had a beautiful and happy family life. We were blessed.

On Valentine's Day, February 14, 2018, I sent my children off with special treats. I put diamond earrings in Alyssa's ears. I remember touching her ear and seeing a smile light up her face. There is something special about giving our daughters their first grown-up gifts. She was wearing a black and white dress. I felt so proud looking at her, this beautiful girl, inside and out.

I kissed her as my hands left her ears and told her I loved her as she scooted out the door to school.

A couple hours later, I had just finished playing in a tennis tournament when I got a text message that stopped me in my tracks.

"Shots fired at Stoneman Douglas High School."

"Kids running and jumping the fence."

I felt an immediate sense of extreme loss throughout my body. I grabbed my purse, ran to my car, and drove as fast as I could, running several stop signs. A rush of loss and pain penetrated my blood, and I knew in my bones that something was terribly wrong. I kept calling my husband in the car, using automatic dial until he finally picked up. I was screaming at him about a shooter in the school, just screaming, until I arrived near the school but couldn't drive all the way in because there were so many police cars blocking the way. I abandoned the car up on top of the sidewalk, grabbed my purse, and ran toward the school. As I reached the middle school, adjacent to the high school, I saw yellow caution tape everywhere and tons of police officers with huge guns. There must have been at least a hundred kids and parents, scurrying around, shocked and stunned by the whole scene.

Everyone kept saying there was a shooter in the freshman building, where Alyssa was a student. I pulled up her schedule on my phone, trying to figure out where she was at that exact moment. Alyssa's best friend, Abby, came running up to me. I searched her face before focusing on the space on either side of her where Alyssa should have been, as those two were normally together, literally inseparable, like best friends at that age often are.

"Where's Alyssa?" I said.

"I don't know!"

This wasn't a good answer for either of us. *Panic.* A few minutes later, Abby got a text message from somebody saying that Alyssa had been shot. I fell to the ground and started to scream. Then I jumped up and ran toward the school, but police officers pushed me back. I yelled at them that my daughter was shot and asked which hospital she could have been taken to in an ambulance or a police car. They sent an officer with me, and I just ran, faster than him at first even though he appeared to be in better shape than me. He caught up and put me in the back of his police car. The seat was cold and the air around me was hot. We arrived at a nearby Marriott, which appeared to be set up as the reunification center, but nobody was there yet. Once inside, I called different hospitals, trying to locate Alyssa. As I left, I bumped into a complete stranger who offered to take me to one of the hospitals. He drove too slowly so when we came to an intersection I jumped out and found a policewoman and told her where I needed to go. She directed me to a large, heavily muscled officer, who took me to his car and drove me for about half an hour to an area hospital.

Why are his lights not on? This is an emergency. I need to get to Alyssa right now.

When we finally arrived, I ran into the emergency area and looked in one of the rooms. I saw a girl with long black hair and thought for a second it was Alyssa, but as soon as I ran toward her, I realized I was wrong. Someone put me in a room to wait. I asked them to check the operating rooms, just in case, but no luck. I left with the police officer, who was so big he could barely fit in the car and I directed him back to Stoneman Douglas High School because I realized Alyssa must still be there—I had tracked her phone to that location. She never went anywhere without her phone, and it indicated she was at school.

He said he needed to take me back to the reunification center at the Marriott. Everyone there was running around, trying to figure out what had happened. Someone told me they were looking for Alyssa. When my husband and his parents and my parents arrived, authorities kept putting us in these designated spaces, like, if you're trying to find your child, go here. They kept moving us, until we ended up in a bigger room where they brought in piles of pizza boxes and bottled water.

I was freezing in a tank top. Someone wrapped a Red Cross blanket around me. At one point, I went to the bathroom and fell to the floor, screaming at the top of my lungs, just screaming without any possibility of controlling myself.

At that point, I could feel in my body that she was gone.

I don't know how time passed that day, but from when I got that first text at 10:30 in the morning, somehow it became eight o'clock at night and we still had no confirmed news. About two hours later, I spoke with Rabbi Mendy Gutnick from my synagogue, but he didn't know anything, either. It wasn't until two o'clock in the morning that we were taken into a private room where an FBI agent said that he didn't want to speak in front of me, that he only wanted to talk to my husband.

"No," I said, "you're going to tell me, too."

The agent told us that Alyssa had been shot in the face and that she was unrecognizable, which turned out to not be true. This was the most traumatic moment I could ever have imagined and this professional from the FBI didn't know what he was talking about. What he said was a lie or a mistake. I had no idea in that moment, but finding out like that was so wrong and so irresponsible of him, especially after we'd been waiting for so long for any kernel of information. How could the FBI get that so wrong?

For hours and hours, authorities had been asking us for pictures and names, and we kept e-mailing them and they kept losing the information and putting us through the same process over and over again. We signed more paperwork and left.

I picked up my mom and we headed to the medical examiner's office. Nobody told me I could go or suggested it, but I just went. I told them who I was and they came back with a photo of Alyssa. That was the first time I knew with 100 percent certainty that she had died.

They shared that photo but they wouldn't allow me to see her because they were still preparing her body. I had to sign paperwork to release Alyssa to the funeral home. My husband and I went there to start planning her funeral. Two hours later, we were finally able to see her. I remember touching her with my hands, trying to warm Alyssa's body, trying to bring her back to life. Her body felt so cold. I didn't know what else to do. I looked at where she had been shot, where the bullets had gone inside her ten times—in the hand, the top of her hand, and her heart, and other places. I asked the attendant for a pair of scissors because I wanted to cut Alyssa's hair. I didn't want them to take everything from me. I thought that, if I could keep some of her hair, then I could still feel like I have a piece of Alyssa with me.

A video from the day of the shooting shows where the shooter broke the glass window in the door before shooting into the classroom. Alyssa was in the direct line of fire and the video shows the shooter going across the hallway and coming back, which is when he killed her. What it didn't show was Alyssa screaming, which is what I was told by her friends.

By the following day, my emotions were all over the place, but most of all at that point, I was angry. I wanted to go to a local park where people were gathering. I told my husband I had something to say even though I had no idea what it would be. I went right up to the first reporter I saw among many lined up to catch whatever scoop they could. I told her who I was and that I had something to say and she just brushed her hair off her face and said she wasn't on the air. She just brushed away her hair, like whatever. I went down the line of reporters until I found one with a microphone and I told him I had something to say. He handed me the mic and told me I'd be on air in fifteen seconds.

I don't remember what I said, but I know that it launched me on my way to advocating for school safety. Even that day, in the immediate aftermath, filled with unimaginable pain, I knew I had to do something.

The next week we spent at home, sitting *shiva*, a Jewish ritual of mourning when you're supposed to stay home with family and friends to mourn your loss. Countless people came to our house and they kept saying the same thing. "We want change."

"Great!" I'd say.

"But I can't do it," I kept hearing in response, again and again.

"All right," I told them (and myself), "I can."

I didn't sleep for the next three months. As a visual learner I need to write everything down or draw it, so that's how I tried to deal with everything. That's when I came up with the idea for Make

Our Schools Safe. It was my way of dealing with my pain, to try to fix what I could, to try to make change.

A couple weeks later, I enlisted a couple of lawyers to help get it off the ground. I went up to New York City with some students and we went on the *Today* show on NBC and did a CNN Town Hall and a few other news programs. I wanted to make immediate change. I needed to know I could make a difference, which meant I wanted my voice to be heard.

I wanted to honor Alyssa and her legacy, and that desire still drives me. I want her friends to live for Alyssa, to breathe for her, because I know that is what Alyssa would have wanted and that's exactly what's happened.

Shortly after our trip to New York City, I decided to try to make a direct impact here in our county, so I ran for the school board, largely on a platform of school safety, with a focus on creating accountability so that our students could flourish and enjoy the benefits of a top-notch quality education. All children should be able to go to school each day without being afraid of getting shot. Parents should feel sure that they can say goodbye to their children in the morning and hello again at the end of the day.

I raised more than $120,000 for my campaign and ended up winning around 65 percent of the vote. I'm a competitive person, and when I set my mind on doing something, I do it. Of course, this whole campaign was about much more than me and I think that resonated for a lot of families in our county.

I am living proof that your voice is your power.

I believe in that completely and when I have something this important to say I will not be silenced—not by institutions, government bureaucracy, or misogynistic men who think that a woman's place is in the kitchen. I just won't accept that. I'm not going to stop, and just because I'm a woman, it doesn't mean I can't do something. I *am* going to make a difference. I *am* going to make a change. I am going to be heard and I will *not* be silenced.

We started a 501(c)(3) about two years ago, with my husband, friends, and colleagues, and recruited a social media expert who runs our website, a qualified CFO, and a safety expert who has been a valuable consultant for how we approach our strategies.

Our mission is to empower students and staff to help create and maintain a culture of safety and vigilance in a secure school environment. We want to drive and guide best practices in school safety. We want to coax schools into using proactive measures and adopting methods of being prepared, like if you see something, *send* something. Mental health is a huge aspect of keeping schools safe. For example, we must aim to have a good ratio of mental health counselors for students, and reactive measures, such as having silent duress buttons in school to be used as a direct link to law enforcement, to get them on-site as quickly as possible.

We've focused a lot of our effort on the state legislatures. A year ago, we were able to get Alyssa's Law passed in New Jersey, where I was born and grew up. Citizens and politicians had been trying for five years to pass this law, which is all about the duress button, but Governor Chris Christie kept vetoing it. The tragedy at Marjory Stoneman Douglas High School changed that and when we called it Alyssa's Law it was received with a different level of acceptance. People knew that we simply had to do more by creating layers and layers of protection to ensure that our kids are safe. We never thought that something like this could happen to us in Parkland. New Jersey residents felt the same way and when enough of them made it clear that they wanted to make this change, Governor Phil Murphy signed Alyssa's Law. We were obviously ecstatic!

Our advocacy through Make Our Schools Safe is what moved the needle. We reached out to all the legislatures, bringing this to their attention, telling them in no uncertain terms that if this law had been in place on February 14, 2018, it might have saved lives.

I'm working now in Tallahassee to get Alyssa's Law passed in the state of Florida. We are actively lobbying legislators, trying to get them to make it a top priority during this legislative session. We've passed one level and are moving toward the next, on our way to the governor and making it the law of the land.

I feel like I'm getting in their faces, and the more they hear about it, the more I think it's going to rise to a level of importance in both parties and get passed. To keep this alive, I reach out to the media every week to let them know what's going on with Alyssa's Law. It's important to keep them aware and maintain our momentum. If they want to do a story on Alyssa's Law, that's great because it brings our cause to the public; the legislatures need to listen to their constituents. I keep asking my friends to e-mail and call their legislators to stress the importance of Alyssa's Law. So far it's working well, and I will not stop until I make it happen.

Besides this campaign, a big aspect of our organization is what we call our Make Our School Safe clubs. We also call them Dream Team clubs because we want students to create a culture of safety in their schools. So far, we have about ten clubs that have started up around the country, like the one in Stoneman Douglas High School. We feel that if the students create a culture of safety and feel comfortable—if they see something and *send* something—then we can prevent suicide or the next school shooting.

Kids know what's going on in their own schools. They see things on their phones. They know who's who, so we want them to feel secure and be able to report anything suspicious to law enforcement with the simple push of a button.

All of this work keeps me plenty busy and for the most part I am able to stay focused and keep pushing. There are those days every once in a while when I feel paralyzed with grief and loss. But I know I have to get out of bed and change the world.

What keeps me on track is Alyssa. She lives in my heart, and whenever I begin to waver, I hear her talking to me: "Just keep going, Mom."

I feel like I can't stop. I'm on a mission. There's so much that needs to be done and I'm laser focused to keep Make Our Schools Safe going because our message is clear and we are sticking to it so we can make real change. If we try to expand what we're aiming for by dabbling with other aspects of gun violence prevention, then our message gets foggy and diluted and people get confused. It has to be crystal clear.

We want to focus on school safety because it's not polarizing. We all can agree that it's not a partisan issue, Republican or Democrat. We all send our kids to school and we all want them to come home alive. At the end of the day, test scores don't matter if that doesn't happen. You can be the best at this or that but if you're afraid to go to school, what's the point? It doesn't matter if you're rich or poor or black or white. Bullets don't discriminate. We need to make sure that every school is safe and I want to be a part of that. I want to create that change in as many states as possible.

I go to schools all the time and connect with the students. We just had a "Rally to Tally," where I took kids around the capitol in

Tallahassee to meet the legislators. Working with students is a huge part of being a school board member; they give me hope that we can make things happen.

When I was a kid, my soccer coach always told us the same thing. "You get knocked down; you've got to get right back up."

I took that message to heart then, and it still drives me now. Whenever the pain knocks me down, I remember how important it is for me to get back up and keep going with my mission. It's also important to focus enough on self-care, so I try to take time for myself and of course my family. If you have experienced anything that has taken the wind out of your sails, then it's vital that you still take care of yourself, through exercise and eating right and maintaining moderation in your life.

Your mental health is key to all of this. Receiving therapy, pretty much from the day this all happened, has kept me focused and functioning at a high level. Being consistent with that is helpful and I can't emphasize enough how important it is to seek help and see a mental health therapist of some kind. Our overall health and well-being depends on being able to talk about our problems and to process our grief.

Sometimes it's just a matter of getting back on the horse after you fall off. I had an older and a younger brother so I learned at an early age to fend for myself. Now, with two sons of my own, I've become a role model for them. Knowing they look to me for how to act and react to this whole thing, I try my best to be strong but also honest in letting them know it's okay to grieve and to communicate the pain and loss they are feeling.

Everyone deals with this process differently and individual faith plays an important role. I am Jewish, but until February 14, 2018,

I wasn't particularly spiritual or religious. We observed major holidays, like Rosh Hashanah and Yom Kippur, at the synagogue. On the night this all happened, our rabbi was with me while we were waiting to hear something concrete about Alyssa. I told Rabbi Gutnick that he should start planning funeral arrangements and he told me no, have faith. I told him again that he needed to do this and he assured me that he had my back.

In that moment on that day, he was there for me as my rabbi. I needed to know that he supported me because as a mother, I felt that was my duty. I gave birth to Alyssa; I raised Alyssa; and now I felt that, as her mother, one of my last duties would be to bury Alyssa.

The next day, when I knew for sure she was gone, I went to the nearby Everglades. I felt like that was the closest place where I could be with God and ask why this had happened. When I left there, I picked up my mom to bring her to see Alyssa at the medical examiner's office. I looked up at the sky. It was orange and bright and the sun was penetrating. In that moment, frozen in time, I felt that Alyssa was at peace, that she was okay. I'm not sure that I felt at peace, though, because at that time I felt as if I were on drugs. I had never taken drugs, but I could just imagine because my head was spinning and everything felt surreal.

I took a photograph that day of the orange sky and it's become the visual anchor of our website. It's a tangible reminder to me of Alyssa, like her hair, which I keep in a glass box in her bedroom. These are my guiding lights, and they will always accompany me on my mission.

P.S. FROM MICHELLE

I knew from the get-go that I wanted to have a mom in this book who had dealt with the unthinkable tragedy of school violence. Who could be stronger than that? I was sitting in my living room one week before the manuscript was due and as always I knew it would come to me. I just had a feeling, like I'd experienced with every other story. I was focused on the mom who grabbed the microphone during a CNN piece and challenged our president after the Parkland shooting. How could I find her? I looked her up online and in one simple phone call, which she herself answered, we spoke right away like old friends do.

Lori said she would be honored to be in the book. Truthfully, I am the one who is honored that she took the time to share her story. Her faith in her daughter's presence in the orange sky was one of the most profound moments during my interview. It reminds me of this verse:

SO WE FIX OUR EYES NOT ON
WHAT IS SEEN, BUT WHAT IS UNSEEN.
FOR WHAT IS SEEN IS TEMPORARY, BUT
WHAT IS UNSEEN IS ETERNAL.
(2 CORINTHIANS 4:18)

God bless Alyssa and Lori and may they both be a part of many beautiful orange skies.

#What Is Your **GRACE?**

SPOOKED

Being diagnosed with cancer rocked my world. I was a basket case of anxiety, panic, and fear, pleading for my life, begging God to send my mother to watch over me. Leveled by the pain of surgeries and chemo, I sought the help of a hypnotherapist who specialized in meditation and stress reduction. She taught me how to calm my body and mind.

During a weekend of rest in the mountains, I decided to try out my new meditation skills. I lay on my bed, relaxed my entire body, and set my intention on healing and communing with God for reassurance and faith. As I flowed gently into another state of consciousness, I released the tight grip I had on my body, allowing a "held" memory to come floating to the surface.

On my fifth birthday, I was sitting around our antique kitchen table in my warm and loving home with several friends, munching on cake and playing with balloons. My mother handed out old-fashioned Charms suckers, perfectly round and flat, in a multitude of colored cellophane wrappers. I remember her making sure that I received a specific blue sucker. A moment later, we were asked to open our suckers and I received the prize.

"You are the lucky one!" the wrapper said.

Of course my mom orchestrated it all and I felt very special.

The symbolism of this memory smacked me in the face as I meditated. After thirty-five years, this was thrilling, but the implication of the memory was also spooky. I had prayed for reassurance and felt as if my mother was letting me know I would be okay, by reminding me that "You are the lucky one!" As reassuring as that was, it still spooked me a little bit.

What spooks you?

4

Bonnie Carroll:
HEALING LOSS FOR
MILITARY FAMILIES

A daily routine of prayer is the ultimate game-changer.
As you begin to pray consistently,
you will notice other parts of your life
opening up in healthy ways you never anticipated.

—Allen Hunt
Dreams for Your Grandchild

MEET BONNIE CARROLL

When I initially decided to write this book, I wanted to include a mom
who was brave enough to speak about her involvement in the military,
and who used that experience to provide support to other families in
similar circumstances. I thought of my friends, Maryanne and Melinda,
both of whom loved their sons to the moon and back but had to say

goodbye to them when the boys went off to fight for our country. As a mother with three boys, I cannot imagine what it must feel like to be out of touch for days or weeks at a time while your own flesh and blood are in a war zone somewhere far away—prepared to make the ultimate sacrifice—and knowing you may never see them again. I don't know how I could manage that.

Once I found out about Bonnie, I was not surprised to feel simpatico with her. The first thing she told me was that her life had been punctuated by loss. Yep, check. She lost her mom at a young age. Yep, check. She is committed to healing a community she knows firsthand. Once again, me, too. Check, check, check.

Bonnie Carroll is a military veteran, the surviving spouse of Brigadier General Tom Carroll, a former staffer in the Reagan and Bush White Houses, and the president and founder of the Tragedy Assistance Program for Survivors (TAPS). She founded this program following the death of her husband in an Army C-12 plane crash on November 12, 1992.

Her efforts, along with those of the dedicated team she has put together, have made TAPS the leading national military service organization, providing compassionate care, casework assistance, and 24/7/365 emotional support for those impacted by the death of a loved one serving in the military.

Bonnie retired as a major in the U.S. Air Force Reserve (USAFR) after a thirty-year career, including service as chief, casualty operations, Headquarters, U.S. Air Force (HQ USAF). Her last assignment was on the HQ USAF National Security and Emergency Preparedness staff in the Pentagon. Prior to joining the USAFR, she served sixteen years in the Air National Guard as a transportation officer, logistics officer, and executive officer. Bonnie also served in Baghdad, Iraq, as the deputy senior advisor for programs in the Ministry of Communications, where she managed funds for the reconstruction of the telecommunications capability in Iraq, the modernization of the postal service, and the creation of the Iraq Communications and Media Commission. She continues to work with Iraqi surviving families facing traumatic loss.

She has dedicated her life to serving our beautiful country. I've always wondered if people outside the military really understand the freedom and independence these families afford us. It's staggering when you consider the extent of their sacrifice. We don't have to look too hard to see evidence of it all around us every day.

Bonnie's life epitomizes these qualities in spades. She was moved by the mission of our book and signed on without hesitation. I barely had to lift a finger, a sign for me that through God's grace I am simply facilitating His work.

Without needing to explain much, we bonded over a shared sense of losing our moms and how that affected us growing up. When Bonnie described how she jumped into real work, I was taken in right away. She tried to compete at a professional level in the equestrian world and worked two or three jobs at a time to make everything work. The perfectionists who hired her taught her an amazing work ethic, which reminded me so much of exactly what I went through making my own way and starting from the bottom. I had many jobs before I graduated from college — strawberry picker, cannery worker, fast food, Denny's hostess, deli worker, cashier on the college lunch line, video rental clerk, and finally I settled into retail at Macy's and Nordstrom, where I developed a love of clothes I still enjoy today.

Bonnie showed such tremendous promise that she kept getting plucked up by one hiring manager after another, propelling her forward to the next gig and then one better than that. This led to her being selected by President Ronald Reagan to write for him in the White House.

Before serving in Iraq, Bonnie was appointed to be the White House Liaison for the Department of Veterans Affairs (VA) in Washington, DC. Prior to that position, she served as director of the Tragedy Assistance Program for Survivors (TAPS) and ensured the development of programs to aid military families coping with a traumatic loss.

I could write an entire book on Bonnie but let me whittle it down to the major themes about her that speak to me so strongly.

I have always believed that you don't have to bear children to be a mom, and this is the case for Bonnie. I am convinced that she has become the "mother" of all of her TAPS families, and I'm quite sure they share my sentiment. Starting long ago when her mother inspired her to go into the military, to meeting the love of her life in General Carroll, Bonnie has exemplified what every child wants in a parent, and even though her dream of having her own biological children did not come to fruition, I believe that the love she shared with Tom became the foundation of TAPS, making Bonnie a proud mother of the many military families she has guided through seemingly insurmountable losses and grief. Over the course of her lifetime, Bonnie has woven a beautiful tapestry of positivity and expanded our concept of genuine motherhood.

I'm honored to present Bonnie Carroll, a 2015 recipient of the Presidential Medal of Freedom, in her own words.

My parents were politically active and living near Washington, DC, which provided me an opportunity to volunteer with the Republican National Committee. I threw myself into the job, so much so that a couple of days later someone asked me if I was looking for a full-time position. I ended up with a young firm that had just orchestrated President Reagan's successful campaign, which turned into a tremendous platform for me to meet people involved at the most senior levels in politics and campaigning.

After a year of working hard to build up their firm, which was a wonderful experience, I joined the National Guard, the reserve of the Air Force. My mother served in the Army Air Corps, so at the age of twenty-six I figured if I didn't do it then, I never would. After six months in basic training and technical school, I came back to Washington to continue a medical career.

I ultimately wound up working in the White House, first on a commission and then on the Economic Policy Council, focusing on domestic issues. My first assignment was to respond to a letter President Reagan had received about the Tennessee Walking Horses. This trickled down to me because people knew I had an equestrian background. I wrote the letter for President Reagan, describing in the best way I could, how he would feel, and a couple of days later, I got a call from Howard Baker, the chief of staff at the time.

"Bonnie, President Reagan read the letter you wrote for him, and he loved it, and we want to know if you would like to move over to the West Wing and write for the President."

I wound up working for about one and a half years on cabinet affairs, crafting decision memoranda, correspondences, and fact-checking presidential remarks.

President Reagan introduced me to my future husband back in 1988. Following the campaign between George Herbert Walker Bush and Michael Dukakis, we heard about three gray whales that were stuck in the ice up in Point Barrow, Alaska. Their plight caught on, mesmerizing the world long before we had spectacular things like that go instantly viral.

Tom was in charge of the international operation to rescue the whales, which also became a global effort to build peace and understanding. One evening, President Reagan stopped by my office on his way to the Residence.

"Bonnie, aren't you in the National Guard? Well, there's something on television that has to do with the National Guard and some whales up in Alaska. Call someone you know and find out how we can help."

This demonstrates what was so beautiful about Ronald Reagan, that he was always asking, how can the government serve the people and make the lives of citizens better?

That night, I called someone I knew who connected me to someone else, and someone else, and someone else. Eventually, someone in Alaska said they'd call me back, and when the phone rang it was two o'clock in the morning and it was Tom, calling from Point Barrow. We fell immediately into a flowing conversation about the whales and the president, and oh, my God, I had this indescribable feeling in the middle of that call, like, *Who are you, and where have you been all my life?*

I ended up going to Alaska as "the girl who worked in the White House," and met Tom, the celebrated Army guy, in person. Right from the start, each of us felt as if we'd always known each other. In fact, when I asked him where he had been all my life, he answered quietly, "I'm right here."

We had agreed to marry before we even met in person. All of our phone calls and letters led us straight to it. The whale rescue occurred in October 1988, and we married in 1989.

Tom had custody of his daughter from a previous marriage and we tried desperately to have children of our own. When that didn't happen, we opted to do foster care. When Tom was killed in 1992, we had three teenagers in our house, including Jordan, who had just graduated and enlisted in the Army.

When I think back to that day and look at the tragedy in hindsight, it's amazing how I had some kind of precognition in the three days leading up to Tom's crash when he was killed in a small executive plane that the military used for transport. In this case, he was flying eight people to see a visiting two-star general to show him what the Army Guard in Alaska was doing.

They crashed on a Thursday. The Tuesday before I was sitting at my office in downtown Anchorage, working for the Department of Law there, when all of a sudden I felt an overwhelming sense of panic. I jumped up from my desk and said, "I've gotta go; I've gotta go!"

I jumped in my car, raced out to the base through a falling snow, completely sobbing, and went directly to the person working at the hangar.

"Where's the plane? Is it here?"

I was hysterical. The plane landed just fine. Tom came into the hangar and I ran to meet him, as if he'd just returned from the most dangerous bombing mission imaginable. I was a wreck, gasping, unable to breathe.

"I'm okay," he said. "I'm okay."

The next morning, Wednesday, November 11, Tom was speaking at an event in a big armory. He was the commanding general and had done many of these speeches before, but just as he went up to speak, he leaned over to tell me something. "I'm going to do something different."

He spoke about what it would mean to give his life for this country. I was just sitting there, in tears, and couldn't figure out why I felt emotional.

If he had only known . . .

Tom was killed the next day.

Crash.

Gone.

The morning of his death, as Tom and I were on the way out to the hangar, he called out to the girls, who were stuck in their room doing whatever it is that teenage girls do. "Bye, I'm leaving, love you!"

Nothing. He said it again, still nothing.

"Well, we've got to go."

Just as we're about out the door, one of the girls called out. "We need lunch money!"

They had clearly heard him. He went downstairs to talk to them and was being polite and respectful and communicative—all the things a dad tries to be with blooming girls. I saw Tom look at them a little longer than usual, and all of a sudden, he just melted down.

"I could die in a plane crash today and you would feel bad," he told them.

"Tom, don't you ever say that," I said. "Why would you say that?"

He had never said anything even remotely like that before. It was so out of character. He stood up and grabbed the girls.

"I can be upset but I still love you."

When we got in the car, he kept tearing up.

"Tom, what's going on?"

"I just want to make sure they're okay," he said, "and that they're going to be okay."

At the hangar, as the guys were getting ready for the flight to Juneau, they were all talking about their lives and families and things. For some reason I couldn't grasp, it was not just the trivial banter I'd heard them exchange so many times before.

A week later, to the day, to the very hour, I was sitting in the same chair for Tom's memorial service. A military crew had been filming an event a week earlier and had left the staging intact, complete with a big American flag and all the trimmings.

I really think precognition exists but not at the conscious level. It's not something where somebody says, "Don't drive today because you could be in a car accident," or anything like that. You're not aware of it until you look back. In the moment, you're just responding to a feeling. We all have some kind of timeline in life. That was Tom's and that was the day, and at some level, he knew that.

The day of the crash was a beautiful one. The Alaskan sun was shining where I was in Anchorage; we had no idea how different it was down in Juneau. Everything that could have possibly gone wrong did. The ground navigation system was broken, which Juneau didn't know. The pilot and copilot weren't indicating well in a white-out snowstorm, and their instruments were telling them they were over the runway. They radioed that they were going to dive down and land on the runway because their instruments told them that's where they were. So they actually dove straight into the mountain, even as they were transmitting. They knew where they were and that their communications had stopped.

The first word I got was that they had lost communication with the plane, but there was still tremendous hope. Someone from Tom's staff came into my office. He was so kind and gave me lots of reassurances. "Bonnie, please get home so we can monitor this."

Two hours later, I was home when a three-star general, the commander of all the armed forces, came to my house. By then, we knew that it was a different story. He said that they didn't know where they were, but that the plane had to be on the ground somewhere since it would have run out of fuel by then.

We went to the armory where the families had gathered. I felt a collective mix of deep upset, random hope, and prayers—all overlapping each other until finally they found the plane, climbed a rope down to it, and discovered that they'd all been killed.

Some kind of amazing shield went up in that moment, as if it were protecting me from the magnitude of the loss, allowing me to ease into the grief.

When General Jimmy Doolittle spoke about his son James Junior's death at the age of thirty-eight, he said something wonderful, "Until it fully settles in your soul that you will never see this person ever again, do you really mourn the loss?"

Now I know, through all the work we've done with 100,000 family members and counting, that the real mourning begins about six to eight months afterward. This is almost impossible to explain to someone, but that's how it works in most cases.

On November 12, 1992, I picked up a phone and called friends, family, and Tom's mother. I said the words. I said the words to tell the truth.

"Tom was killed in a plane crash and you have to come."

I went through all of that, repeating the facts, but from the outside in. It wasn't until that summer, six to eight months later, that the facts came from inside out. I walked into the house one day and it was quiet, and it just hit me.

Tom's daughter, Mikey, my stepdaughter, went right away to her biological mother, which was not a good situation for anyone. I had to fight for her to even stay for her father's funeral, which was more than difficult. Mikey wound up going with her sister who was struggling with several issues. We went from having a full house of five people, with my dad staying with us quite often, to the two of us. That made it even worse. Without Tom and the girls, the house became unbearably quiet. I was suddenly a widow and mourning the loss of the unborn child we had been hoping someday to have, to add to the wonderful family we had put together. Almost overnight, all of this joy turned to grief and the one person I thought I had to turn to was gone, leaving me with layer upon layer of loss.

I kept working throughout all of this for the Alaska Department of Law and I was also still in the Alaska Air National Guard. Tom was killed a week after President Bill Clinton was elected. Since all my credentials were in Republican circles, I knew my résumé wouldn't get me very far in Washington under a new Democratic administration. I stayed in Alaska, where I had great friends, a job, and a house.

I was busy working, but by the next summer, my grief had become overwhelming and the emptiness was just debilitating. I became a broken record to my trusted friends.

"I can't go on. I can't live like this. I just can't go on without him. Tom was my everything, my whole world, and now it's gone," I broke down to a trusted friend.

The shock had worn off; the ceremonies and remembrances were over, and well-wishers had receded into the background, as the world around me resumed its normal pace. Finally, one of my closest pals gave me a real slap in the face.

"Knowing how much this hurts, and how painful it is," she said, "would you rather have never met?"

This triggered such a visceral reaction in me. I snapped from flight mode right back into fight mode as I defended my memories of Tom and our love, and I must have talked until we were both exhausted. I had no regrets. I just wanted more time. I was greedy. I figured even ninety more years could never be enough. That's when I realized that I had to take the love Tom had left me and pay it forward. It wasn't long before I turned this into my catalyst for creating a triumph out of tragedy. I was certain that I could find my way through this, just as I had done after my mother died.

I reconnected with some of the other eight widows from the crash who had stayed in the area and we became really close, which was so helpful. If we laughed or cried, it didn't matter. Everything was acceptable with these other women who really understood and held no judgment.

Having these kindred spirits is so important. I have been there and I know what healing looks like. It's simple: "I see you. I'm here to help."

Because of my job in the Department of Law, I was on the board of a local group called Victims for Justice, helping to support people who had lost loved ones to homicide. I went to court with what we called homicide surviving families and helped with the process. I was also involved with the families of police and firefighter survivors and discovered the amazing support systems they set up for one another.

I had no idea what empathy really meant until I encountered these peer support programs.

After Tom was killed, I came to wonder where the support was for all of us military widows. I had assumed support groups existed for military loss, but over the course of the next two years I found that there were none. This became the inspiration for Tragedy Assistance Program for Survivors, or TAPS.

Tom held two positions at the time of his death: deputy commissioner for the Alaska Department of Military and Veterans Affairs, and general of the Alaska Army National Guard.

I was accomplished professionally, too, and was used to being in leadership positions but didn't know where to start in forming a support group. Finally, I found potential support within the government and in the private sector, and Bill and Hillary Clinton became huge supporters and remain involved to this day.

It certainly helped that my husband had been a general and that I was a military officer, with experience at a senior level of government. As a commander in the Air Guard, I understood military culture. I'd had two of my airmen die, one to suicide and one to a heart attack, and I'd been through family loss. With all that background, I knew that if I didn't act right away, then somebody else would come along.

My proudest accomplishment with TAPS is that we now have children who initially came to us as babies in strollers and we have had the opportunity to be involved with them through every stage of their childhood—with a community of military kids, all developing coping strategies together. I now have half a dozen who are still involved and have become legacy mentors, reaching back to the next generation.

Perhaps this has been my legacy for children everywhere. Even though I've never had one of my own, I've been fortunate to impact the lives of so many children, and that keeps me going all by itself.

My mother was a tremendous influence in my life. She was the reason I joined the Air National Guard. It was so important to her to serve her country. She was an extraordinary, vivacious woman who was so gracious. I hope she can see what I've done in the shadow of her legacy. Her memory drives me, along with my love for Tom.

Years later, Hollywood came to Alaska when they made a film about the rescue of those whales. It was called *Big Miracle*, starring Drew Barrymore, and it was based on Tom Rose's book, *Freeing the Whales*. Dermot Mulroney played the character based on Tom and Vinessa Shaw played the one based on me. I became an extra in the movie, which took a year to shoot and came out in 2012.

When they were filming our wedding, which is how the movie ends, they kept that scene playing in the background as the credits rolled, with no audio. The director told Dermot to make a toast to Vinessa, although no one would hear it. There I was, a wedding guest at my own wedding, listening to "Tom" declare his love for "Bonnie."

"When we spoke, you asked me where I had been," he said, "and I said, 'I'm right here, waiting for you.'"

Everybody who knew the real story, and saw me right there, began bawling.

I went up to Dermot afterward.

"What made you say that in that way, in the present tense?"

He looked at me, crying.

"I don't know where that came from."

When Tom and I met, we didn't waste time. We grabbed our love for each other and rode it for all it was worth.

I recently had a call from Billy Ray Cyrus, who told me he is making an album.

"Bonnie, your husband, Tom, came to me, and he wants me to perform the song that was written for you on this album, called 'Love Lives On.'"

That sums it up right there. That love drives me every day and I know that Tom is just as much responsible for TAPS and all the healing we provide as I will ever be.

P.S. FROM MICHELLE

Amazingly, there was no organization like TAPS when Bonnie first thought of starting one. She spent two years searching for a model, figuring one had to exist somewhere, but none of her amazing Rolodex of friends and colleagues in Washington had ever heard of anything remotely close to what she envisioned.

When we finished our conversation, it was clear to me that Bonnie's mom had given her a special gift when she exposed her daughter to the military, which inevitably inspired Bonnie to pursue that life.

Bonnie and Tom could not have children of their own, but you don't have to give birth to be a mom. Bonnie proves this on a grand scale. The healing she provides has given birth to an exponential number of children.

She understands that we can help those who need healing if we have experienced tragedy and trauma in some shape or form ourselves, that top-down support is fine and good, and we need people to write checks. But when we can sit side by side with those who are hurting, or even better, prop them up from below and inspire them, then we can reach to the heart of the matter and recognize and do what is urgently needed to help people heal from tragedy.

Moms like Bonnie are the backbone of what we do. She is a fighter, a lover, and change agent who operates from a place deep within her soul. The evening after we spoke, I watched *Big Miracle*, one of my favorite movies. Just as I got to the scene where Bonnie and Tom met, I got an e-mail from Bonnie, sending me photos from her life with Tom and the filming of the movie. I e-mailed her right back and I can't wait to hug her in person and thank her for her service.

#What Is Your GRACE?

FEAR

My hypnotherapist, Connie, was professional, loving, nurturing, and beautiful! During my cancer treatment, she helped me transform my grueling physical pain in ways I never thought possible, without pain medications. Normally, we need to build up our white blood count in response to the debilitating effects of chemo. To help with this, I received a routine shot of Neulasta. Along with the positive effects came a slew of nasty side effects, and for me the bone pain was intolerable. Each week, Connie helped me overcome that by focusing on healing.

She was so patient as I cried and agonized over my fear of dying. I felt sorry for her because I kept rehashing the question of my chances of recovery like a broken record. Do I have a 70 percent chance survival rate or is it 90? I was obsessed with the math. From the beginning, Connie had a clear sense that I would be okay! Instead of being hung up on what she could or could not say because of the threat of being sued, Connie spoke from the heart, which seemed so centered and connected to the Spirit. When we focused on breathing and feelings, she asked permission to place her hand on my arm and spoke to me quietly during the meditation.

By the fourth week, as I studied her face more and more, I began to have an inkling that Connie resembled someone. When I opened my eyes from a meditation, it hit me. Connie looked exactly like my mom would have, had she lived! She had the same shape of face with identical jet-black hair and the same piercing blue eyes. It was uncanny. Connie was born the exact same year as my mom, too. We marveled at the support that God brings when we are open to it and release our fears.

What are your fears?

5

Debbie Moak, Bridget Costello, and Marianne Gouveia: THE ENDLESS ROAD OF ADDICTION

*I learned that courage
was not the absence of fear,
but the triumph over it.
The brave man is not he
who does not feel afraid,
but he who conquers that fear.*

—Nelson Mandela

MEET DEBBIE MOAK,
BRIDGET COSTELLO, AND
MARIANNE GOUVEIA

Like thousands of other adolescent children, Debbie and Steve Moak's teenage son struggled with drug addiction. During their family's journey, from the initial stages of denial through eventual intervention and recovery, they learned that sharing their story was therapeutic for themselves and extremely helpful to others.

In 1999, Debbie and Steve founded notMYkid, Inspiring Positive Life Choices, to expand these possibilities. Today, their organization provides a variety of youth programs designed to help kids make positive life choices. To date, the Moaks have impacted more than 1.3 million kids throughout Arizona, and we are all excited at how they have furthered their mission by helping families in all fifty states.

Bridget Costello and Marianne Gouveia know this territory all too well. They have experienced what no mother or father should ever encounter, and what none of us can ever be prepared to handle. Both of them lost their sons to the disease of addiction. But instead of letting that tragedy contract their life, which would be perfectly understandable, they have chosen to expand their presence in the universe, by the grace of God and through their commitment to helping others in the midst of similar circumstances or trying to survive the aftermath of their loss.

Getting to know Debbie, Bridget, and Marianne has been a blessing for me.

When my firstborn son was really young, I hovered over him, like many mothers do, consumed with protecting this innocent child from any harm or bad things in this world. If there was something to worry about, I was quick to identify it, and I didn't miss many opportunities to fret and fuss and ponder all the possibilities of things that could go wrong with my child.

When Debbie Moak showed up at our school to speak about her organization, I was all ears, even though I could hardly imagine anything like that happening in such a nurturing environment. But when she described what notMYkid was really about, and shared stories and statistics of how many kids are being sucked into a world of addiction and all the dangers that come with that territory, I realized that my family had no guarantee of being immune to these possibilities. It made me wonder: What if anything like that should ever happen to my son?

Debbie's mission was to educate and prepare kids for not if, but when, they would be confronted with the lure of using drugs or alcohol. She had another program to talk to them about creating a safe environment for those facing depression and/or anxiety, and she invited parents to come in with their kids to meet with their peers and their parents to gain a better understanding of what was going on and what they might eventually face.

Debbie was actually the first mom I approached almost fifteen years ago to sit down and talk to about what she's accomplished and how she's inspired me. Initially, as a first-time mother with visions of making a difference in this world, I was so anxious to explain to her what I wanted to do. First because I didn't know her well, and also because she had already overcome such a personal battle with her son and accomplished so much in the founding of notMYkid.

As I listened to the story of her beautiful son and his battles with addiction, I couldn't help but develop a clear picture of what that would be like for me and how I might deal with such a remarkable and seemingly all-too-powerful challenge. Debbie's grace and confidence were so inspiring, and her connection to her faith opened the door for us to become kindred spirits and instant friends and collaborators, which we have been now for years.

When I met Bridget and Marianne the energy and common purpose were quite similar, as each of them has embraced their own affinity to Christianity and God, which has not only carried them through their loss, but has invited them to help so many others in need.

What began for me as a terrible fear of what could happen to my son has morphed into a call to help all boys and girls facing the vulnerabilities of growing up in today's world where too many drugs are so readily available and incredibly dangerous.

By the grace of God, Debbie, Bridget, and Marianne have shown me what this world is all about and what I can do to make even a small difference in the lives of families burdened and broken by the ravages of addiction.

For all those who are struggling right now with any of these demons, or who have experienced the awful effects of addiction, these next stories are for you.

I'm blessed to work and partner in the same community alongside Debbie Moak, Bridget Costello, and Marianne Gouveia, and here they are, in their own words.

DEBBIE MOAK

I barely remember being on my knees on the floor of the treatment center in Montana, leveled by unbearable pain and fear, knowing we faced a life and death situation with our son. All I could do was pray to God that this clinic could save him because it was crystal clear that everything we had tried for the past several years had not worked. Still, I felt as if I was letting Steve be ripped away from me, that I was failing him as a mother by giving him over to these people. In the midst of my meltdown, I knew better: his recent experience of being homeless and helplessly addicted would eventually kill him; and we had to force him into this facility, a legitimate, good place with qualified people trained to help. Still, my head and heart were fighting each other, much like the opposing forces that were plaguing Steve, threatening to take his life.

We had no choice! After finally reestablishing contact with him, we knew that we had to intercept his movement and get him to a safe place. Our years of denial, of thinking that this couldn't happen to *our* son, that Steve would be okay, that it was just a phase, were no more. There would be no more claiming that he was different from the other addicts or that he was not capable of being so self-destructive. Up until then, I was still enabling his habits, convinced that we could steer him back to health, that my husband and I could "fix" him. I thought that prayer might do it, that each night when I got on my knees, God would hear my plea for help.

But as I fell to my knees that day in Montana, surrendering to the reality that Steve was a helpless addict, I knew that I had to take my faith to a higher place where God could help Steve accept the treatment that this place offered.

Before Steve began to slip away as a teenager, I was a normal mom of two sons and an elementary school teacher for ten years, a Christian, a devoted wife, and active in the community. I was a champion for underdogs, as I dedicated time to serving kids with special needs. I was strong because of my faith, and from a young age, my dad was an amazing role model for me.

On paper at least, Steve appeared to have everything going for him—good grades, vice president of his class, and a strong athlete. He even went to church on Sundays with no complaints. Everybody liked him. But starting as a young teenager, Steve developed a whole other life that we did not know about until it was too late.

During a field trip in the middle of sophomore year, a beautiful senior cheerleader asked him if he wanted to smoke a joint with her. Over the next eighteen months, we observed all sorts of changes, like moodiness, losing interest in things he formerly found important, general lethargy, and more time sleeping. Through the insidious power of denial, we were barely suspicious and wrote off most of Steve's changes as normal teenage behavior.

"You wouldn't use drugs, would you?"

"Of course not," he said. "I'm an athlete, and that stuff would mess up my performance."

His grades remained good, he kept up with most of his sports, and there were no dramatic changes we could point to as signs of any serious trouble. Then one day, we discovered a home drug test kit, which we didn't even know existed, and discovered that Steve had tested positive for different substances including pot. We were pretty stunned, as this did not comport one bit with our zero-tolerance policy on any type of drugs. So we did what we thought any caring parent would do. We grounded him for two weeks, thinking that would be drastic enough to get him back on the straight and narrow. Of course, we did it all wrong, starting then and throughout the rest of high school, but we didn't know any better. Every parent we spoke to believed that this was the way to deal with it, so that's what we did.

Over the next few years, Steve never really crashed and burned, not like we think it happens as portrayed on TV, and we rode the good and bad times until he began getting more aggressive and quit everything but playing baseball. We continued to rationalize his behavior as well within the range of how boys can be, and we worried about him, but figured he would find his way.

That ended abruptly when Steve came home one night, falling down drunk, which began an accelerated cycle of taking the car keys away, waiting up nights, performing awkward scratch and sniff tests, believing he would clean up, and repeating those cycles again and again, until there was nothing more to take away from him. Whenever we forced him to see a therapist, Steve would get aggressive and smoke even more pot.

We hoped that a change in scenery would help when he went away to college, but we quickly realized that this was a terrible choice. Not only did he take his brain with him, the one that was failing him chemically, but he was in a party school where pot, alcohol, and cocaine were readily available. The change of environment did the opposite of what we had hoped.

Steve's grades were barely decent, but in spite of that he ended up becoming president of a fraternity, which made us worry even more, as he could indulge in whatever vices he wanted. He didn't come home the first summer, and then the drug tests came back positive for marijuana and cocaine and Steve had to leave school.

"You're out," we said. "You can't live here because we will not allow any drugs in our house, under any circumstances. None."

Our choice prompted every parent's worst nightmare when Steve moved in with his drug dealer, a kid he knew from high school. This prompted fighting in our home, as my husband and I had different philosophies on what to do and how to do it; this took a toll on our marriage.

We received constant calls for money. Steve traded away all his clothes for drugs, and stuff went missing from our home. Only later did he share stories about cocaine houses and having guns pulled on him. I tried to engage him and "fix" things, but this only made his father mad, which he had a right to be, since Steve had stolen his credit cards. We couldn't keep track of him, even when he stayed with us for days or weeks at a time.

I was falling apart, living in a sob-fest most of the time, as I helplessly watched Steve slip further and further away into a person I couldn't recognize. We offered to send him to treatment, but we refused to give him any money. I must admit that I would have continued to enable him if my husband had looked the other way, but thankfully he didn't. When Steve exhausted his friendships and had nowhere else to go, we packed a suitcase with the few things he had left and drove him straight to a treatment center.

When we got there, I begged my husband to take Steve home, as the other patients in the clinic seemed so desperate and scary, even though I knew he was as lost and addicted as anyone else there, and that he needed care we couldn't provide. My darkest moment came as I watched them in a room with a collection of coffee mugs hanging on a wall, each one painted by an addict, which represented their stay for treatment. The idea is, you paint a mug as therapy, and after you get out you are supposed to come back a year later to collect it and reaffirm your sobriety. That sounded so optimistic until I was told that the black mugs hanging there represented former patients who had died and never made it back.

I wasn't sure I could get through this, let alone Steve, but I have a strong husband and I hold on dearly to my faith. Both helped me reexamine my role in this, as I did what every parent does, at least for a time: I blamed myself, and when I wasn't doing that, I blamed my husband. Someone had to be responsible, or at least it seemed so. I could manage a roomful of special needs kids as a teacher, but not my own son. Fortunately, my husband and I fought through this and we survived.

We insisted that we were not stinky parents, that sometimes you just can't control things. We prayed together for Steve, and to stay together no matter the outcome. In spite of my initial collapse in the treatment center, I eventually felt a sense of peace as I deepened my relationship with God, finally understanding that He uses everything for our good.

Steve came home six months later and went back to school, got a one-bedroom apartment, and underwent regular drug testing to maintain his accountability. He went to Alcoholics Anonymous (AA) meetings and we did Al-Anon (for families of addicts), as we were still learning so much about this disease and the family dynamics.

We met parents from all walks of life, some with resources and some barely making it. One thing bound us together: love for our children and an abiding fear that they could die because of their addiction. We had to realize that our child had a problem and it wasn't going to end; we can only lay our head on the pillow at night and hope to sleep if we are sure we've done all we could to keep our child as safe as possible, with the best chance to survive.

Al-Anon, with its beautiful and essential support system, helps make that a reality, even for people who are not as fortunate as we are to be able to afford expensive treatment. No matter what financial situation a family faces, parents have to begin with the fundamentals, which means telling the truth because denial is a bigger impediment to fixing the problem than anyone's bank account. I'm not saying that money is not an important factor because it is. But throwing money at a problem without facing the hard, cold facts is a waste of time and energy. Cash will not make addiction go away. It will not cure this disease. Healing is hard work and requires care and dedication, and that's what we learned once Steve came home and tried to put his life back together.

This is not easy at all because in our society people who are addicted to alcohol and/or drugs reside at the bottom of the barrel when it comes to mental health care, and the stigma is strong and alienating.

When the counselor told us that we needed to put ourselves in our son's shoes and see the problem through that lens, this was a big wake-up call. It's not an easy thing, but it's extremely necessary, and now we explain that to all our families. Once they realize they are not alone, that there are countless families suffering through similar circumstances, it helps to move them along to a place of greater empathy and acceptance for their recovering child.

Every parent wants their kid to grow up in peace and live a life full of love and success. The hardest thing for any parent to admit is that their child is dealing with addiction, or a disability, or almost anything not considered "normal" or comfortable or safe. When we give birth, we want—and even expect—that our child will be the best he or she can be, by the grace of God and our own best efforts. With no training to detect or understand most, if not all, of what is going on, the first instinct is to ignore or deny or pretend it will go away. After all, your child is special, so how could anything so bad happen to him? That changes quickly until you just wish your kid could be average to the point of boring, as long as he is safe and sound—and not addicted!

The truth is, Steve *was* mixed up with some bad people who often didn't know him or have any interest in doing so, and he *was* in danger of getting run over by a car or hitting one himself because he was so stoned. He *did* risk getting shot by being in the wrong place at the wrong time with the wrong people.

When I see him now, sober, in his early thirties, married, and a father of two little ones, I am astounded by the change in his nature and how he's become such a kind, strong, and compassionate person.

I sometimes think back to when my husband and I were on our knees in the rehab center, praying for Steve. All we wanted was for him to survive and get another chance to live—without drugs. I didn't have a picture of what it would be like today, when I'm amazed that we are where we are, because this is still a one-day-at-a-time affair. Every time the phone rings now, it triggers an alarm of dread, even for a second, in spite of knowing better.

That's because sobriety is not linear. It's a daily choice, and while I know Steve chooses sobriety every day, there are no guarantees.

We wanted people in trouble to know that they matter. Because we made ourselves stop living in denial, we decided to help other children and families suffering through similar challenges. With our metaphoric PhD in addiction, we contacted everyone we knew who might have an interest in this problem and invited them to our home.

Right then and there, we formed the foundation of what would become notMYkid. We set up our first board of directors, quietly helped with money, and applied for nonprofit status in April 2000.

Our original mission was to tell other families about our story so that they would not feel alone, as we had for so long. One thing led to another, and when we began visiting schools, everything exploded. We outed ourselves with our story, and this did a lot to erase the stigma of families dealing with addiction. People came out of the woodwork to tell their own stories of struggle and pain and loss. The phone kept ringing, and we were astounded to find out how many people were going through similar things.

At first, it was a tough sell to get into our local schools, as they did not want us there, telling the truth.

"We're sorry about what happened to your son, but what does that have to do with us?"

Sadly, his story was being reproduced everywhere. We pushed on, doing presentations with firefighters, in churches, and eventually in the schools, where administrators only needed to look at the data to realize that their students were extremely vulnerable.

It wasn't only substance abuse. We were astonished at how kids came up to us and shared their stories of dealing with depression, bullying, and even rape. Our eyes were opened even wider to the raw human struggles these children were struggling to overcome.

No matter how much progress we make, some people feel that kids struggling with addiction, and their families, should stay in the closet and keep their problems out of the mainstream because there's something "wrong" with them. We take the opposite approach, by leaning into the challenges and embracing the brutal process of acceptance, actionable therapy, and healing. This is the only way to bring addicts and their families out of the dark and into the light.

Many people love notMYkid because our educators know the territory from their own experience. They are honest and edgy and real and, most of all, credible. We never judge or portray anything we don't know firsthand, and we are quick to acknowledge that we are perfectly imperfect. That's what makes us who we are and why so many people come to us for help.

One of the biggest lessons for parents to learn, whether they have children at risk or not, is to accept the reality that you are not in total control. Your child is going to become who they are—not who you think they should be or who you want them to be. This is true, not only in the world of addiction, but it also applies to the world of athletics, arts, or academia.

We preach character and behavioral health skills.

I am often asked to describe the most important things we can do as parents when it comes to dealing with children at risk. Here are a few of them, in a nutshell:

1. Understand that the bulk of tragedy comes from missing the early onset of addiction. Get on the same page as your spouse, as mixed messages make a house divided and it will fall.

2. Set boundaries. Verify. Remember that talk without action is meaningless. Parents must verify report cards, meet with teachers, and review homework. Enforce curfews. Drug testing is imperative and learning how to say "NO" is essential.

3. Talk all the time, and then take action. Talking to your kids about drugs may reduce addiction by 50 percent, but when grades slip badly, or you see other indications of serious changes in behavior, immediate action is imperative.

These are just a few of the keys to finding success. Our biggest focus is on getting people to become proactive and communicate from a place of love. This approach could turn things around within our culture because we now have the knowledge to educate a new generation of children so that they do not have to go down this path. We want to get to them all, by the tens and hundreds and thousands, so we can show them that there *is* a better way.

Steve is proof of that, as he has been working with us now for several years and continues to be a positive and highly authentic role model for kids at risk and the families who love them—one day at a time.

****

BRIDGET COSTELLO

I was raised Irish Catholic, pretty much to the core. I went off to college, met a gorgeous guy, went out with him once, and next thing I knew, I was pregnant. My parents supported me as a new single mom *and* made sure I finished college. They couldn't have cared less about what other people thought, but I felt great sadness that I had fallen short of the aspirations they had for me. My pregnancy was psychologically heavy. But once Conor was born, the light came right back on.

Oh my God, this child of mine!

I met my husband, Blair, when Conor was nine months old. He was the only dad Conor knew until he learned that his birth father was out of the picture, which left a real hole in his life.

Eventually, we got married and Blair adopted Conor. My dad and brothers were wonderful, too, and Conor always had male figures in his life. But who really knows how he probably tried to fill that deep, elusive gap as he got older?

Conor was a rambunctious little boy and always had what is called ADD—attention deficit disorder—today. He was enrolled in the Optimal Learning Center, where children could get up and move around freely to allow them to learn in their own way.

At home, my mother indulged him as only a grandmother can. I was trying to be a responsible parent, but my mother often reversed my best efforts, ignoring my plan to teach him discipline and responsibility. By the time he reached high school, Conor had moved to my mother's and refused to come home. She and my dad were doing what they thought was right, and it was nobody's fault, but Conor was going off the rails. He had an amazing childhood, for the most part, but he started to wreak havoc on our family as he got older. He was a decent kid and had many talents, but he had issues.

I found his journals not long ago, where he wrote about his three F's: faith, family, and football. He was deep for a teenager, but we could tell he was partying at fifteen when he began ditching school. Eventually, he got kicked out, and things spiraled. His biological father had addiction issues, so maybe this played a role in Conor's story. When he was about ten, he wanted to know his biological dad, and they had about five visits. Conor quickly learned that his biological dad was a decent man, but he still had to wonder why he had abandoned his son. What really broke my heart about Conor and his biological dad not being connected is that his biological dad has so many compelling attributes. I still feel tremendous sadness that Conor didn't get to see how cool his biological father was, but then again, his biological dad missed his chance to know his son, too.

I would tell mothers struggling with whether the fathers should be a part of their child's life, that if they're healthy, the answer is yes because all of us need to know who we are and where we come from. That's my one regret. If I could go back, I would have forced his biological father to be involved in Conor's life because, while my husband, Blair, was wonderful, it would have been beneficial for Conor to find a sense of completion or acceptance with his biological dad.

As Conor's bad behavior escalated, I had to leave work all the time to drive around and hunt him down. I'd inevitably find him doing drugs or evidence that he had been. We did treatment programs in the area and sent him to a mountain program, not for punishment but to experience some meaningful personal achievement that might reboot his reasoning. Conor went with a friend and they escaped, so that was a big bust.

That's when a friend asked if I knew about a program for teenage kids where they were locked down in what could be called a voluntary prison. By that point, we were desperate. Police were coming to our house, and we had two little girls we were trying to raise without exposing them to Conor's stuff. I knew that if I didn't do something drastic to contain my kid, then I was going to lose my marriage and my life. We were going to counseling to overcome this, but nothing was working.

"Conor, as your mom," I said, "you have to stay alive, and you have to finish your high school education by eighteen, and it's my job to get you there."

We hired a huge guy who worked with special needs kids to track Conor and keep him out of trouble. He was sensitive and wonderful, but even he couldn't contain Conor, so we called the guy in Montana to come get our son and take him to that voluntary prison. At that point, it was our only hope. Conor didn't know this was coming, but he went missing that night. As usual, I waited up for him, hoping he'd show, thinking that maybe he was just partying too much, and that maybe if we rode out the storm, it would eventually be okay. I was seriously in the denial club, which is natural for parents, but it's the worst place to stay.

At 6 AM the phone rang. It was Conor. He was so high on something that wasn't just marijuana. I listened for an hour and a half. He and his friend were talking about running away to Mexico. I could hear he was at this kid's house, and I figured we could tell the bodyguard to go get him. I felt like God was telling me that Conor had to go away—for his own good and to save our family. I almost backpedaled, but after hearing Conor so zonked on drugs, I knew he needed serious help.

The transporter showed up and scared the crap out of Conor. He thought it was the police, as he'd been dabbling in steroids and selling them and thought the football player he owed money to had sent this guy, which just freaked him out.

My father and I went on the same plane to Montana, but Conor was so high he wasn't even aware we were there. He was sixteen. It was tragic leaving him there.

"Mama, don't leave me!"

"Conor, I don't have a choice."

He was able to finish high school in a self-directed program. That gave us a little bit of joy, but the rest was terrible. The program wouldn't let us see our kid for nine months—until he earned it. Each little setback was a result of some tiny crap that exasperated us.

"God dang it, Conor; get it together, so we can come see you."

We should have had the chance to be united as a family, with counseling from the get-go. Tough love is one thing, but to isolate us like that didn't work.

I still can't think too much about how I put him there.

Apparently, Conor told people there that he was a really good football player. He re-created himself, which was amazing. He got himself back in great shape. He read books, wrote letters, and they believed him, that he was a real athlete. Out of 360 kids there, Conor got to try out for the football team at the local high school, and then attend it and play. He was the only kid to do that, which kind of shows how charismatic he was when he put his mind and body to something positive. They took him there every day, mostly because he bugged them and even begged. We flew in on weekends to watch him play at Thompson Falls High School. All the kids chanted his name—*Conor! Conor! Conor!* He was really good, and he rang the victory bell when they won. He was even featured in the local paper with pictures of him in his uniform.

We figured he was on his way and that it wouldn't be long before he was ready to come home. But he jumped the gun on that and got everyone else to buy into that. We let him leave the mountain program because the local football coach said he could live with him and his wife, and they'd take him to school, which sounded fine to me.

Conor got scholarship offers to two community colleges, and Drake University gave him a shot to come and play. I tried to get him to go there so he would stay away from the people and places at home that represented his unfortunate past. He chose to stay home, however, so we set him up in his own place because I couldn't have him back in the house again, possibly re-creating all the same tensions.

But Conor wasn't ready to be on his own. Someone had always done things for him, whether it was me or his grandma, so he never had to learn to figure things out for himself. It was different with my girls. When Tara was nineteen, she was studying in Italy and her apartment flooded. She called me a couple of weeks later and told me the story; she had taken care of it by herself. When I was nineteen, I had a baby.

My parents helped Conor set up an apartment. My cousin had a construction job for him, we got him a vehicle, and life looked like it was going to be good. Against everyone's better judgment, he brought home one of the kids from Montana to live with him. They say never put two addicts together. They learn things from each other and they're not all good things, either.

On the one hand, Conor was making progress. He was eighteen years old and alive, with a high school diploma, just as I'd asked.

Within six weeks, though, he had been evicted from his apartment. He was back on drugs and had gone to Mexico. And then he lost the car.

For the next six years, we set Conor up as best we could, watched him fall apart, and tried all over again. My husband and I withheld help until Conor promised he'd go to rehab—again—but that didn't work, either. My mother and father indulged him with cars and apartments and whatever else they sincerely thought would help their beloved grandson.

Back then, the opioid crisis was just starting.

"Mom, there's two drugs I'll never do," Conor said. "I'll never do meth or heroin."

He did cocaine, though, and whatever else he could get. When he was about twenty-two, he met a woman at least ten years older who quickly found out that Conor had steady access to cash, and her father was a heroin dealer. They started feeding a prescription habit. Conor would go into a doctor and complain that his foot hurt. Without a blood test or any questioning, he'd get a prescription for more than one hundred painkillers, and he'd take them and overdose. A doctor in the hospital tried to keep him alive. We had one doctor trying to kill him with pills and another one trying to save him by pumping those killers out of his guts.

This vicious cycle repeated itself five times before Conor fell into a heroin addiction, all because of a woman who was terribly addicted and had no one helping her.

I sent Conor to a program in Antigua that accepted people who were destitute, which he certainly was at the time. We paid what we could and visited him a month into his stay.

A month later, when we picked him up, he looked beautiful. But that same night, he went back with that woman and they drove straight to her dad's house.

In hindsight, you need to have an opioid program. It's not the same as alcohol. It's a specific addiction. It takes a long time to fix, if it can be done at all.

Soon after, we organized a family vacation and Conor came along. He had always ruined other vacations, but this was just a couple of days. It seemed almost normal again, watching him mess around with his sisters, blinged-out in his sunglasses, and showing off his tattoos.

"Mom, what kind of jeans do you think I should wear?"

I hadn't had that kind of conversation with him in years. I felt a sense of calm and peace, with an optimism that had been missing since he was a boy.

But Conor was loaded with a staph infection, which we didn't know. The night before he was to go to another rehab in California, he sat at the foot of my bed, promising me he would get through it and come home healthier than ever.

He was already suffering badly from a diseased body and God knows his mind was diseased by this point, too, from all the drugs he had taken. I never knew if he was or wasn't crazy because he was never off drugs long enough to experience who he really was, at his core. He was hanging with such shady people, too, which only made him less himself.

While he was in the California rehab for thirty days, he received twenty-five prescriptions for drugs I never knew existed. Then he came home, used once, and died. That was it. He used heroin only once more and he died. Conor had five overdoses in the last year of his life and the last one killed him.

That's Conor's story. He passed eleven years ago on August 21, 2008, when he was twenty-four years old. It took me four years to feel like I was even breathing or thinking or doing anything remotely normal. I had two fourteen-year-old girls at home, so I had to deal with their lives and their grief from losing their brother. I was in a fog of my own and second-guessing everything I had done or not done when it came to saving my son.

I didn't see it at the time, but there was a sense of mercy in Conor's death, for him and our family. Everyone had suffered for so long. With addiction, the hardest thing to do is not to blame anyone and we did our best not to fall into those traps. All we could do was help one another heal, although I could not conceive of healing as a possibility, not at first, at least not for myself.

I was astonished that the rest of the world continued on with its daily activities. I kept wondering, *how is this possible*? *Don't they know? How could they not realize that Conor has left the universe?* It felt as if nobody knew except me. The world just kept going, in spite of my pain and the emptiness I was experiencing.

What really hit me was the clear feeling that I didn't want the world to forget him. Conor's life meant much more to me than his drug addiction and death. That said, I didn't want another family to ever experience this kind of loss.

Conor was multitalented, from his musical abilities to writing, and he was a great athlete, too, especially football, which he loved. Those passions meant more to him than the drugs, but in the end, they couldn't save him from the addiction. Nothing could, not even our love.

My mother brought this up recently. "You know, I was just trying to keep him out of the system or off the streets."

"Mom, it's okay," I said. "He might have died earlier if you hadn't been there."

For a mother, tough love feels counterintuitive. Experts tell you to let your kid sleep on the street or in the car; I did that sometimes because I had a buffer in my mom, who always took care of him when I put my foot down. If she hadn't been there, I probably would have indulged him even more. Either way, it was lose-lose, and I knew I never wanted another mother (or father) to experience the pain and loss I still feel today.

Somehow, I had to turn Conor's life into a win-win.

When I came up with the idea to create the For the Love of Conor Foundation, a donor-advised fund through the Arizona Community Foundation, I was focused on helping children develop their passions, hoping that would raise them higher than any drug could do. Many children don't get to enjoy sports, at least not enough, so I started with that concept: that Conor's life should help people benefit from the things he enjoyed, even if those people were foster kids or homeless or underserved because all of them need to discover the joy of their passions.

I've been a nonprofit fundraiser for years, after a career in education. My perfectly Irish father was the founder of the Saint Patrick's Day parade in Phoenix. I went from teaching to staying home with my children, to planning this event, which meant supervising thousands of people and working with several committees and communities to bring it all together. I did this for eight years as my first nonprofit gig.

I invite my friends and my family to our large annual event, and every year I am overwhelmed to discover that addiction has touched every single family. Whether you're wealthy or impoverished, old or young, it has affected everyone. It doesn't discriminate.

I didn't want to start another nonprofit. I'm so blessed now because the Arizona Community Foundation has allowed me to raise donor-advised funds for the work I do now, providing arts programs for abused children.

Several years ago, on the anniversary of the night Conor passed away, I glanced at my phone at two in the morning and saw an e-mail from a friend, telling me that I needed to know about this organization called Mother's Grace and its founder, Michelle Moore. "You two need to meet."

She didn't know it was the anniversary of Conor's passing. I wrote back. "First of all, what are you doing up so late? It's amazing that you are making this connection for me tonight, of all times. Did you know it's the anniversary of Conor's death?"

When Michelle and I met, we quickly realized our lives aligned on a number of issues, including worshipping at the same church. I always do this novena from Knock, Ireland, that prays for families. On August 21, 1879, there was a miracle in Knock, where the Virgin Mary appeared. This is now a shrine. This was the same date as the anniversary of Conor's death. I discovered a specific novena designated to be recited between August 14 and 21, which focuses on the healing power of families. Michelle loves novenas and does them all the time, so she was so into this. Needless to say, meeting her and becoming involved with Mother's Grace has been a deep blessing for me. I wished I had known her when he died.

Starting when he was sixteen, I carried a small life insurance policy on Conor. He was always so wild, and I wanted to be able to have a funeral if he should pass away before me. The policy was just for $25,000, but I accidentally paid it twice, which meant we had the most amazing funeral to celebrate him, with trumpets and beautiful singers and a big party that we staged in a ballroom at the Mondrian Hotel in Scottsdale, the hip place to go at the time, and a place that Conor loved.

No matter what, I wasn't going to let the world forget Conor. I was blessed to have the money to do this for him, and it ended up being just what I needed, too, to allow me to grieve and provide an outlet for everyone else who loved Conor.

Throughout these years of healing, many incredible mediums have come to me with evidence that Conor is still with us. This provides hope for a mother who's lost a child. My family didn't want this to become public, but I had to do my thing, in the form of the foundation. It took me four years to be strong enough to do it, and we are still working on projects today.

His birthday is always hard for me. That's why I have a celebration each year on January 14th; we have a luncheon and invite children's charities we are helping. I ended up being connected to J. D. Hill, a former NFL player who founded Catch The Vision (CTV), an all-volunteer nonprofit that supports the work of The Phoenix Dream Center, which provides transition housing for homeless, chemically addicted people. We've had musicians from Alice Cooper's Solid Rock foundation perform, which was amazing. Every year, we find new charities to support. We've also supported Parents of Addicted Loved Ones groups because resources are still lacking in that area.

Meeting Debbie and Marianne has been wonderful for me, as only a mother who has been down a similar road can truly understand the depth of pain and fear that come with it.

On the last night of Conor's life, a guy named Mike, who was in the witness protection program, called me at two o'clock in the morning and said the words I'll never forget. "Conor has died."

The whole family woke up and we went to the address Mike had given me. A woman stopped me inside the apartment and said two things to me. "Let us do what we need to do, and we'll call you when you can come back and see him." She was a cop. I was too confused to answer.

"Bridget, I wouldn't want to see my son like this."

They wouldn't let us see Conor, as they didn't know if it was a crime scene. I went home and took her advice and didn't go. I just waited to see him at the morgue. I always regret this because there were writings and maybe pieces of music he was creating in his room. I didn't get any of his stuff, his clothes or anything.

Mike never called me to come get Conor's stuff. I never heard from him again. He didn't come to the funeral and the heroin addict girlfriend didn't come either. The good people in Conor's life showed up, though, and that made a difference.

One day, eight years later, on Conor's birthday, just when we were having our special luncheon event, my mom told me about a police officer who had come by her house. Apparently, she had been looking for me and left her card on my door, which I found when I got home.

I soon realized she was the officer from that night who had told me not to come back. She had told me the night he died that she knew Conor a little, that she had been called to the apartment another time and knew he was a good kid, just badly messed up with drugs and the wrong people. Here she was calling me eight years later.

"Hi, this is Natalie, a service officer for the City of Scottsdale. I have one of your son's things, and I need to get it to you. Here's the number; go to this place, and they'll give it to you."

I went to a huge warehouse, which looked like a museum of drug paraphernalia from all the things the police had seized. I told a lady that my son passed away and she said she was sorry. I said it was okay, that it had been eight years. We were being so polite about such an ugly, awful thing. A policeman standing behind me asked for the number I needed.

"Conor Costello," I said.

"I got it," he said, and disappeared into a massive cavern. It was weird that these endless rows of shelves and boxes stored the remaining possessions of human beings, as if they could be still alive with so many memories. I had no idea what I was waiting for, but I couldn't move, transfixed by the spectacle of the place and why I was even there.

"Did you know you contacted me on his birthday?" I said.

"I just looked at this wallet and had to get it back to you," he said.

To me, this was Conor's final message, as if he were speaking to me. "Mom, I'm here and I'll always be with you."

"This wallet was the physical property of your son, which was processed the day he died. It stayed in a little box here for the past eight years, just the wallet."

It was an Ed Hardy wallet, stylish, like Conor. There was a crumpled dollar inside and his ID because he couldn't have a license at that point. Conor could look Irish or Italian or Israeli because of his dark and curly hair. I also found a gift card to a store. I keep the wallet with me, and it still triggers a profound feeling.

"It's okay Mom. I'm here."

We are an incredible community of survivors—Debbie, Marianne, Michelle, and many others. I feel so fortunate to walk in the shadow of their grace, and they continue to bring me comfort as I cope with the empty space in my life.

It's all coming together.

* * * *

MARIANNE GOUVEIA

My son, Eric James Gruler, was a daredevil who liked the adrenaline rush of jumping off mountains, flying down hills on his bike, and swimming with sharks in Mexico. He was artistic, charming, and witty, with a heart of gold. He shared that with others through his sincere smile and contagious sense of humor. As a practical joker, he liked tackling adults, like his stepdad, whom he'd wrestle to the ground just for the fun of it, which always overtook Eric with happy laughter. He loved doing magic tricks for kids, too, especially when they responded to something funny.

Most of all Eric loved his family and we were his main priority. In fact, Eric had a tattoo on the back of his arm that read "Family." He was very loyal. He often said that he would take a bullet for someone he loved. He was always there when someone needed a hand.

Eric had a profound and abiding love and respect for people with special needs. He grew up with a brother, Joey, who has Down syndrome, and a special auntie, Ann Marie. He often spoke out against stereotypes, prejudice, and negative attitudes toward people with special needs. People like these brought out a special, loving glow in him, and he always appeared to be so happy being with Joey or Ann Marie, just sitting and listening and supporting them both.

While a senior in high school, Eric had a serious wrist injury. Multiple doctors and several surgeries left him with tumors in his ulnar nerve and a gimpy hand. Being crippled as he was, Eric was guaranteed an unrestricted supply of opioid pain killers, which did their all-too common evil and led to heroin use.

We know how this story can go. As sweet and caring as Eric could be, the heroin simply consumed him. Eric often said that heroin was like the devil stealing his soul. He fought hard to resist it and submitted to numerous cycles of detox and rehab, up to six months straight sometimes. Then he'd enjoy another year of sobriety before something would happen, triggering a relapse. Through all of his struggles and the associated burdens of shame and guilt, Eric battled the odds to remain the young man we knew and loved—full of hope and promise—only to end up submerged all over again in a realm of darkness. With those he loved, especially his cherished family, Eric was a protector, but when it came to his own life, he wasn't able to figure out how to protect himself.

We tried everything aimed at reversing his behavior, but as we realized—maybe too late—the situation was out of our control. As we watched Eric slip further and further away, we struggled with helplessness. Despite being determined to stay positive and hopeful, the truth was, on many days, feeling empty from worry and fear, we were just happy he was still alive.

That was our daily goal—to keep him alive. This wasn't just about keeping him off drugs; it was because we had a child with a mental illness, with suicidal ideations. For years, we gave him money, put him in and out of rehab, and took him to doctors, believing that someday it was going to get better and Eric would be okay.

I suffered through an emotional kaleidoscope of guilt and remorse. I was not in denial and even though I did not always know what to do, I was willing to accept that we had a life-threatening problem and had to try whatever we could to fix it. I wasn't a good candidate for the tough love approach, like throwing your kid out on the street to sober him up, because if I had done something like that and it had killed him, how would I have survived?

Of course, questions persisted. Did we go to the right rehab? Should I have gotten him there sooner? Should I have done this? Should I have done that? The list of should-haves was endless. I came to the conclusion that the list of things I was doing right was bigger than the list of things I did wrong. I could only focus on showing Eric unconditional love.

Surrender happened at some point, accepting that not everything was in our control, no matter how smart we are, no matter how much money we have in our bank account, no matter how much we're loving and open and intelligent. When it comes to a disease, and this world of addiction and chemicals and the brain, we have to surrender to the fact that there is no one person, no one, who can be in full control of that.

As Eric continued to spiral, I told my husband, Greg, that I just didn't think he was going to make it. You kind of know it in your heart, like lots of things moms know in their heart, and dads, too. We didn't want to accept the fact that maybe our child was not going to make it, so we worked extra hard to keep him alive and doing relatively well.

For a while that worked, and then it didn't.

Eric chose to end his struggle on February 27, 2016. We miss him every day and thank God for the gift of the twenty-seven years we had with him. We miss his incredible wit and intellect, his joy in having philosophical discussions, delving into the world of politics, discussing the rights and the wrongs of the world, and the good and bad of religion and humanity. Through these endless conversations, Eric let his heart shine for us all to see and feel.

When somebody in your family dies, especially a child, by either suicide or an overdose, it poses a new category of complications that nothing else in life can ever prepare you to face. Not only do you suffer the loss of that child, you have layers of what experts call additional complications related to grief, guilt, regret, remorse, and shame.

You can't go to a traditional support group where you are expected to become part of a community of people who have lost a parent or grandparent due to natural causes. You can't even have a conversation with them because nothing is at all similar in your experience.

Since Eric passed, I am coping with a complexity of feelings and the side effects each one brings, almost like a cancer survivor still dealing with the aftermath of brutal chemotherapy. Only this predicament includes guilt and shame and anger, all of which have to be dealt with in due time.

A lot of stigma remains attached to suicide and drug use. Losing a child flies in the face of any sense of calm one might hope to have, even with the searing pain one feels. When you lose a child this way, a flurry of activity suddenly surrounds you and there is no calm or peace to be found. People are always there, trying to help. They're cooking and cleaning, but they don't know what to say and they can't help trying but they fail, and life is full of chaos everywhere, for weeks, just when you can't handle any of it.

All I wanted was for someone to provide me with a quiet place where I could talk to somebody else who was calm so that I could take a baby step forward and know that there was a possibility of calmness in whatever my life would be going forward.

Inspired by this precise need for calm and understanding, Eric's stepdad and I founded EricsHouse, a nonprofit organization, soon after Eric passed, where we bring people together who have experienced similar losses.

I know the territory. You're splayed open in the crudest way. Your life is shattered into millions of tiny shards of glass, and somehow you have to figure out how to put yourself back together. During that process of rebuilding who you are, all kinds of things have to happen. You have to go back to where you came from, shed some old ideas about who you were, and address the issue of who you're going to become.

In my case, I had spent thirty-five years in the aerospace industry. After Eric died, there was no way I could go back to a boardroom —ever. It became completely meaningless to me. My career had served me well for a long time but going back was an impossibility for me. I needed an entirely new reason for getting up each day, and thankfully it didn't take me long to figure out what I needed to do. I had to find a place for other parents to come, where they could find support in their effort to simply survive the unthinkable.

From the start, we let people know that we don't believe that grief is a thing that needs to be "fixed." When you go into a counselor's office, they say you're depressed. We say, "Well of course I'm depressed. My son just died of an overdose." We don't believe you can fix that. We believe there's a process of grieving and we learn how to address the challenges and difficulties in that process, and then we learn to integrate the loss into our lives in a way that makes sense, depending on the person and their unique personality and circumstances.

We believe that the mourner is the expert in his or her own loss. We just hold their hand with gentle guidance throughout the process and hopefully this empowers people to own their individual experience. That's the only way to get through this type of trauma, by just leaning right into it and being with it. Those who push it away don't get very far.

Imagine a beach ball full of grief that you're holding under the water. When you let go, it suddenly erupts and bursts to the surface. With human emotions, this causes a number of issues in what we could call the integration of grief into your life. We don't want people holding that beach ball under the water. We want it to float so that they can hold onto it as they move through their journey.

People respond to different techniques. It's an unprecedented, humbling experience that can bring you to your knees. We laugh sometimes at this idea of people coming to Jesus, but for some it's quite true and there's substance to be found in allowing yourself to go through a full collapse, surrendering to the deepest pain and grief you could ever feel, beyond anything you might have ever imagined; that's for sure.

You don't have to personify a higher power by identifying what it is or what it looks like or how you communicate with it. The only thing you can control is choosing to aim your path in the right direction no matter what new version of you may evolve, and the only way to do that is through a foundation of hope.

You have to have faith that there is more than this. When you are stuck in a terrible place of unbearable loss, in an empty space that feels impossible to exit, hope is your ticket out of this place. *Hope.* That's about as deep as we go on the religious side, as each of us interprets things differently in the spiritual realm of our senses.

I see one thing similar in people of Jewish and Christian faith, both of which carry so much richness in their traditions. People have learned to rely on them, but I see many moms and dads who get angry with God. One mom screams at God while another embraces the idea of being healed by a higher power. Both reactions are valid. Anger is one of the five stages of grief, so being angry at God and finding a way back to one's faith in a new way depends on each person's individual orientation, which is so baked into who they are. That's something each person has to inevitably grapple with and there is no right or wrong when it comes to this process. That said, being angry with your child is a real emotion. It doesn't mean you don't love your child, but even today, I still wonder: *What happened, Eric? What happened on that night when you decided to take your life? What was it? Whatever it was, we could have worked through it somehow.*

After three and a half years, I am still angry at the fact that it happened at all. Do I direct that anger to Eric? To the world? Neither, really. I just accept it as part of the journey, that I'll probably always feel some anger. It's a natural reaction. I doubt that anyone who has been through this has not felt anger—at the situation, at God, at themselves, or at the one who has died. Those who claim they feel no anger aren't being honest with themselves.

It's also natural to feel guilt or shame about being angry, like, how can I be angry at my kid when he was suffering from this disease? Our approach at EricsHouse is focused on helping people work through that so that it doesn't become something you can compartmentalize and push away because it will come back and keep you from ever finding peace.

Part of self-love is accepting that you're angry. How do you match up an equal amount of love to balance out the anger? It comes through self-love and compassion. You have to honor the emotion because it's real, and over time you can let go of some of it, at least, as you begin to see that there *is* a world after losing a child.

One thing our particular community of parents deals with is the knowledge that we don't own our children. We just don't. We become known as Eric's mom, for example, so involved in caring for our children, raising them and grooming them and protecting them, all as their mom or dad, so when they die, we instantly lose our identity.

I'm not Eric's mom anymore. In that case, who am I? Who will I be, and how do I spend my time now, without him, without the direction that the compass of his life provided? We have to figure out what to do with our time, let alone our identity.

That's what I tell the moms I meet when I feel it's the right moment. If you allow yourself to grow as a result of your loss, you will probably emerge much stronger and wiser and be in a position to help others work through it, too.

A doctor told me: "You need to decide: are you going to let this define you, or are you going to let this experience redefine who you are, and how you contribute and give back?"

For me, I knew I had to get bigger instead of shrinking into my grief. My challenge was, and still is, to find the language to express the facts and the feelings. Every parent who has lost a child has to find a new language that they can own, that feels healthy and real and right. That takes time and practice, and you have to say stuff out loud.

"So how many kids do you have?" a woman asks me at the gym.

"Well, we have five kids. One of them, my son Eric, is in heaven."

I've learned a great lesson from our son, Joey, who deals with this loss in his own special way. He just goes outside and talks to the stars. He says he feels like he gets messages out there and then he brings them back in for us.

"Hey, I saw Eric," he says.

Joey like an angel on earth.

I often keep a light on for Eric at home. We all have our little traditions. Some parents have shrines and fancy setups, which is all fine and good, but we prefer keeping a little night-light aimed softly on our ceiling, which shines down on Eric's picture. Part of my tradition is making sure that this light stays on, as it's become a physical manifestation of the light that shines in my heart.

Everyone responds differently. For me, starting EricsHouse was my only way forward. It just came to me one day. I remember sitting in my office, stuck in a job I didn't care about anymore, going gray, and I just sat up and announced this to myself. "I'm going to start a nonprofit and call it EricsHouse."

Up until then, I had spent a lot of time going through phone records, trying to figure out what had happened. I had talked to Eric at 10:30 that night, and we made plans to have breakfast the next morning. He died at 1:30 in the morning. What happened between 10:30 and 1:30 that caused him to do that? He had prescriptions for more than 500 Oxycontins. That buys a lot of heroin. Eric didn't look like a heroin addict or act like one, but something happened that night between 10:30 and 1:30 that made him decide to take his life.

I found him the next morning. He wasn't answering his phone, so I got angry and drove over and let myself into his apartment. I discovered what I was so afraid of, what I had been fearing for a long time, what I still struggle to speak of, even now, as words can only state the facts of what I knew, that my son Eric was dead.

I started searching for answers. What the hell happened? I made spreadsheets. I went everywhere I could think of where there could have been a connection to Eric. I started seeing mediums. I went to a three-day retreat, which we now run here in Scottsdale, which was transformational for me. I was burning off the pain. I was not going to be the type of person who stays in bed all day because I come from a competitive, aggressive industry in the aerospace field. I just said one day, "We're going to do this thing," and we did.

There's no training manual for this, nothing to explain the amount of trauma and post-traumatic stress disorder (PTSD) that comes from what I saw. I had the image of finding Eric in my head, playing over and over, and every time that image came, I experienced trauma. I finally went and did eye movement desensitization and reprocessing or EMDR, a treatment for PTSD, which was extremely helpful. This is why we eventually get to the point of telling people that they need a team of healers to be around, surrounding them and caring about them.

"We hold your hand until you're ready to let go," we like to tell our parents, and when they're ready, it's because they are moving into a space of healing where they're ready to actually get healed. For many people, this is the only way through it.

There's so much great work being done in the prevention space and many of our clients are affiliated with organizations trying to prevent suicide and addiction, God bless them. But that's not where we are. We're in the *post-vention* space. We're asking a different set of crucial questions, informed by our own experience and what we've learned along the way.

It's an uncomfortable place to be, figuring out what to say to someone who just lost their child. Often, you can't say anything. Even having gone through it, I can't say, "I know how you feel" because I don't know how *you* feel. Your grief is unique. In fact, that's the one thing I can say in this moment: "I can't imagine how you feel; this is horrible. I remember how I felt when we lost Eric," but that's about all I can say.

The fact that I am physically there for them, that I appear reasonably together and healthy and sane, is a small but vital piece of proof in that first meeting, that they can acknowledge that my staff and I "seem pretty normal," and that maybe they can get there, too.

We're good role models. Just for them to see that we laugh is hopeful. That's not something to be underestimated—hope. It's all we really have, along with our faith, to carry us through from one day to the next.

I know I'll never be the same, and I've come to accept that, but replacing those shards of broken spiritual glass is feeding my soul and the point is not to replace every single shard because some will never come back. My loss cannot be disguised or covered over. I may use a Band-Aid to get through my healing, one step at a time, but the real work is deep inside me where Eric still resides, and where I am constantly renewing my faith in this good life, dedicated to finding a new pathway to joy and healing.

P.S. FROM MICHELLE

Debbie, Bridget, and Marianne illustrate the experience of great tragedy, challenge, loss, and grief—the kind where you are not sure you will make it through. But by the grace of God, along with prayer, resilience, and perseverance, each of these wonderful women has found a way to share their experience. When they expose their most painful, searing moments when they were on their knees, we are right there with them, seeing what they felt like in their worst moments.

When we open our hearts to their situations, we may come to understand their loss in bigger ways, allowing us to support their healing, even indirectly, from a distant spiritual place. For some of us, this brings comfort in knowing that there are others going through what we may have experienced, and that there are resources to help us survive and eventually thrive.

Sometimes, it's as simple as if they can do it, we can do it, too. That doesn't mean everyone will start an organization like notMYkid or EricsHouse, but thank God, Debbie, Bridget, and Marianne are doing the work they do, dedicated to such needed services.

#What Is Your GRACE?

LOSS

Connie gave me the most significant support I needed during my cancer journey and maybe in my life. She did not know a lot about breast cancer, or cancer in general, but she showed up for me every week for a year and a half, listening and guiding me so gracefully.

One day, I received a phone call from a friend of Connie's, who wanted me to know that Connie had been diagnosed with breast cancer and was being sent to MD Anderson Cancer Center in Houston, one of the best in the country.

I felt sick, as if I had been hit by a truck. This beautiful woman, a picture of health, who had brought me back to my mom, both with her resemblance and her empathy, was now diagnosed with what I feared most for any woman.

Connie passed away quickly and all I could think of was here I am, still alive and trying to thrive, knowing another blessed woman has been taken and I am okay, ready, willing, and able to pay it forward for someone else.

Do I think God may have given Connie my breast cancer? No, of course not, but I do think there are many spiritual messages and divine symbolisms in my journey with her, and I absolutely believe that God answered my prayers and led me to this woman who supported me in the most divine way, like the mom I needed most. God knew that Connie's final journey was coming, and He put us on a path to intersect, so I could benefit and understand His divine mercy and grace! Now it's up to me to make the most of that blessing.

How do you handle loss?

6

Sister Mary:
ONE LITTLE NUN FIGHTS
POVERTY IN INDIA

Grace will take you places hustling can't.

—Unknown

MEET SISTER MARY

About two years ago, I was just hopping out of church when I got a phone call from my dear friend Delcia, telling me I needed to speak to a priest visiting from India who had heard that I do philanthropic work. Father John Murray was representing a nun, named Sister Mary, who ran an orphanage in a small, impoverished town near Calcutta in northern India and desperately needed money, supplies, and support of all kinds. She was housing ninety young girls in squalid conditions, using one room to feed, school, and care for these girls. Each day, with only minimal resources, they were keeping these girls hidden away from kidnappers and protecting them from disease. Any time one of them got sick they were taken to a local hospital twenty minutes away in a rickshaw, which, considering the roads and traffic, could take nearly all day. I was leveled after hearing of the death of one young girl because it took so long to reach the hospital and she died on the way.

Naturally, I was struck by this set of facts. Although our support services at Mother's Grace rarely reaches beyond our shores, I couldn't imagine my sick child having to endure a daylong trip to a hospital, let alone what it would do to me, someone who has to remind herself every day that speed limits exist for our own protection.

I soon found out that Sister Mary is a force to be reckoned with and that Father Murray could not return to India without securing funds for medical transportation. It's exactly that energy and stubbornness that has enabled Sister Mary to help so many young girls in a country where resources are limited, especially for children cast out of society.

I traveled to India to see for myself. The minute I met Sister Mary in person I knew that she was one tough cookie. She traveled by bus all night long just to come meet me, stopping at a city market at 4:30 in the morning to pick up fresh flowers and greet me at my hotel. She looked beautiful and had a joyful glow surrounding her, even though she had not slept. Her excitement, bubbling with purpose, was contagious from the start. On the long drive north, I could see her wheels were spinning as she meditated on the next steps of her huge project.

At one point, she tapped me on the back and said, "Michelle, I don't feel well. I need to stop." When we pulled over, she vomited on the side of the road, but then she popped right back in the car and began writing again in her notebook.

It's incredibly inspiring for me to consider the details of Sister Mary's *story. Here is this beautiful nun, assigned to a youth hostel for girls. Coming from a nice middle-class life in another part of India, she's placed in a tribal setting where I'm sure she felt uncomfortable. She made this assignment her own by studying the tribes who live in this part of the country, and befriending them by creating ties with the mothers and leaders of the villages. Before long, she convinces them to bring their girls to the hostel to live so that they might avoid enslavement and have a better chance at a real education and a better life.*

She took these children on as she would her own. Like a true mother, she's thoughtful and disciplined, so that these young girls can grow up in an environment where they will thrive and become young ladies. She could have stopped there, but she wants more. So she finds a way to raise money and take on a major architectural project for the sake of these girls.

I was so curious to find out why Sister Mary was doing all this. She is about forty years old, although she looks more like twenty. She has a beautiful, big, wide smile with pearly-white teeth. She is filled with grace, forever hardworking, and always thinking. I never saw her without her little notebook because she's always thinking of the right things to do, taking notes, and making a plan. But along with her constant serious-ness and hard work, she is also precocious and funny. She makes jokes and smiles at her own humor. This highly educated, well-spoken woman is forever serving, serving, serving. I still chuckle when I think of how uncompromising she is in her devotion to her work, always driving forward, yet with an infectious smile.

Meet my favorite sister from India, Sister Mary, in her own words.

I was raised in a good, middle-class family, with six siblings. My parents were farmers who owned some land. In our home, education was made available to my older sister, who then passed it on. So when I was just three years old, I went to live with her so I could complete my studies. During that time, there was a "slow" child in my English class who had some mental challenges. People were impatient with this child and so I sought out the help of a nun. I watched this patient, serene, and peaceful nun proceed to work with this child at a pace slow enough that he could learn in the right manner, and most of all, with integrity and in the right manner.

I want to be like that sister, I thought.

That's when I decided to become a nun, when I was fifteen years old. It became clear to me during an ordination Mass. As the brothers lay on the ground to give themselves to Jesus and get ordained, I made up my mind to become a nun. Even then, I felt like God had a plan for me, and I still do, which means I always follow my heart because I have deep faith that my instinct is confirmation of where I am supposed to go, with the protection and guidance of God.

When I first took over the orphanage, I struggled mightily because that area of India is all tribal, with more than 400 tribes, creating language barriers and cultural misunderstandings. This meant that for a long, long time nothing was getting done at the orphanage and no one much cared.

Before I arrived, I wondered how I would accomplish anything. How could it be possible for me to make any improvements? I had nothing in my head, no strong ideas, no authority, no money, and not much true hope. India is not a Catholic country, so the diocese

I am affiliated with doesn't have tons of presence here and certainly next to no support by way of finances.

Our orphanage had nothing at that time, not even bathrooms, so the children were subjected to filthy conditions and prone to serious, life-threatening illnesses, such as tuberculosis. Whenever the children did get sick, ailing enough that we knew they needed legitimate medical attention, we had no way to get them to the hospital. This problem was our chief priority when Father Murray was sent to America to raise money so we could purchase a Jeep, so the girls could get to the hospital safely and securely when they became sick. You see, up until that time, they had to travel by rickshaw through perilous traffic and dangerous conditions because this part of India is full of bandits and criminals who do not discriminate—they will attack people for even the smallest morsel of food. Even worse are the human traffickers who actually steal young girls and boys right off the street to sell them into prostitution or other horrible forms of slavery.

It seems that Michelle bonded immediately with Father Murray, making a clear and meaningful connection as soon as they met. I knew that Father Murray could have this effect, as he is a saint in priest's clothing, but I was so pleasantly surprised to hear about Michelle's open heart and her willingness to jump right in and take care of things with real, consequent action. Unfortunately, we are not used to this type of "no-nonsense" behavior in India, and Michelle's energy and proactive attitude were unbelievably welcome. In fact, I am still astonished at how easy she made everything for Father Murray and for all of us here in India.

For Michelle and her colleagues at Mother's Grace, all this really required was for Father Murray to describe our orphanage in detail and the challenges we were facing back then, barely three years ago.

He told Michelle about one little girl who had contracted tuberculosis, which had begun to infect her brain. Sadly, we did not have the proper transportation or the financial means to get her to the hospital on time, and she died on the way.

Michelle wasted no time in responding to this story, which I must admit was not the only instance of our children falling so ill and dying. She went to her fellow board members and they immediately agreed that a Jeep would be a good investment. They organized a pipeline for getting the necessary funds to Father Murray, who would be able to ensure that we actually *received* the Jeep, avoiding the corruption that often plagues transactions of this kind in India.

Soon after this, Michelle and I became friends using WhatsApp, which became our lifeline over the next year for exchanging ideas and laughter and great hope for the future. She was quick to develop strategies for assisting our orphanage in other ways, such as repairing issues with our housing and hygiene, which were so fundamental for our girls.

It wasn't long before I invited Michelle to come and see the work that was already being done in our orphanage, with the direct help of Mother's Grace. They had already changed my life and the lives of my girls, beginning on that Sunday in church when Michelle met Father Murray, our "agent" of the Lord, and became the American ally we so desperately needed. It surely didn't take Michelle very long to "get" what Father Murray explained to her about his mission to help an Indian orphanage for girls.

Like most of us, I have doubts about whether God is with us always, but I always come back to my faith because He is always here for me, and I believe He brought Michelle and I together through His grace and the charms of Father Murray.

In the spring of 2017, Michelle and her dear friend, Angela Scott, came to India. Michelle admitted that India was *not* a place she had ever wanted to go. I still laugh when I picture her flying all the way here and getting into a car with complete strangers to drive more than six hours north to see our humble project where ninety children (at that time) were living in one crowded space, sitting or sleeping on rugs, if they were lucky enough to avoid a cold, concrete floor. They each had a thin blanket and a box that they pulled out at night to sleep on the floor—without pillows or cots—and as you might imagine, it can get cold sometimes in this part of the world. In the morning, the makeshift beds were put away so that our one modest room could be used throughout the day for a variety of activities.

Imagine, too, all of those girls sleeping in one crowded room and some of them coughing and sneezing, infecting everyone else until the whole orphanage becomes sick all at once.

As I said, up until that time, when someone got really sick there was not a medical facility anywhere nearby and we did not have bathrooms, either. We had to take the girls outside to a neighboring field to go to the "bathroom" because we did not even have an outhouse, and we used to tie their hands together with string and walk out of our building as one unit to be safe and avoid kidnapping. That's because there was always a risk of being abducted by local criminals, who might take me away from the girls and then gouge out their eyes so they would become beggars, or sell them, or carve away their liver or harvest their kidneys to sell to the highest bidder on the black market. We were always very cognizant of these threats as we took the girls outside each day to relieve themselves.

Along with my other sisters, we were also constantly dealing with young menstruating girls. Having to deal with that out in the fields invariably created sickness and disease, not to mention a distinct lack of comfort.

Michelle admitted that she was nervous about going so far away, out of her comfort zone, but I knew deep in my heart that this trip would be wonderful for her in ways she could not actually anticipate. Perhaps I could feel that it was her calling, beginning with meeting Father Murray one Sunday not so long ago after a morning in church. And just as I suspected, our "crazy" India was quite an adventure for Michelle.

Our social worker and I met her and Angela in Calcutta, a six-and-a-half-hour bus ride from our little village. Even though we had traveled all night, we went to the market and picked up loads of fresh flowers and made some amazing leis and bouquets to bring with us to her hotel. After all, Michelle's journey was much greater than ours. I think she saw our greeting to her as quite ceremonial and it was emotional for all of us. That morning, we went to breakfast and got to know one another a little bit more. Then we headed back to the village by car, with Michelle and Angela squeezed in for a bumpy ride with relatively total strangers.

As we approached home, we kept calling to let the other nuns know we were getting close, as they had a whole presentation to get ready for Michelle, with dancing, singing, and flower garlands to greet them as we arrived and walked toward the convent. When we entered the facility, we washed their feet to welcome them. We held a Mass and a song presentation and presented our two guests with gifts. It was quite amazing for all of us.

Later in the evening, when Michelle saw where she was going to sleep, she began to cry. "I don't think I can do this," she said.

We were inside our little cement block room with metal cots and a single sheet for each of them. We now had a bathroom that was not really a bathroom. It was like an outhouse. Michelle and Angela were tired from the long trip and a twelve-hour time difference, and I could tell she had reservations about our accommodations. As she told me later, "I wanted my Posturepedic mattress, Ugg blanket, 700-thread-count sheets, and air conditioning set on low, blowing directly on me for ultimate comfort."

I knew this was uncomfortable, but we tried out best to be gracious and do beautiful things for these two wonderful women. I hoped our joy in having them would be contagious so that they could feel our gratitude for their visit. We prepared food on hot plates for all of our children and our guests. We had no stoves, microwaves, or ovens. That night we ate an entire meal, prepared on a single hot plate. I knew it was a lot for Michelle and Angela to ignore their own usual needs and embrace our lifestyle. I could sense that they were cautious about eating our food in such a meager atmosphere, that it raised a question of hygiene and health, especially because they could see that so many of our girls were sick and sharing the same food. But Michelle fell for our beautiful girls, sick or not, even though she struggled when they were so eager to hug her and kiss her because she was afraid to catch their colds and flu and even lice.

Both women admitted that they had been told to be careful with eating some of the food and drinking the water. But even though we are a poverty-stricken little convent, with stained walls and garbage lined up outside, we strive to keep the inside of our building clean and tidy. What we cannot offer in physical beauty or comfort, we make up for with open hearts and a joy to be alive.

As Michelle told me, "This is the cleanest dirty place I have ever seen."

I laughed and reminded her that she'd already taken a leap of faith, and to keep an open mind. She ate what we offered her to eat and slept where we directed her to sleep. In that respect, everything went without a hitch. Michelle never got sick and none of her fears came true, and I can say with modesty and good humor that it was a beautiful experience.

God brought us together to love and inspire each other. Michelle even tells me about her love-life issues now. This just shows that we all have the same heart and want the same things for the children of our world.

We are two different women, living at different ends of the Earth, yet our souls have collided in the best of ways. We are both strong women and our wheels spin with our great shared desire to do great things. We are both on a mission to get projects done and we both work hard to accomplish our goals. Today, Michelle and I have a great deal of respect for each other and we call each other best friend.

It's a bit funny—a businesswoman from America, a mother of three boys, befriending a nun from a remote part of India, who plays the role of mother currently for 135 young girls.

Now, I am waiting for Michelle to return and visit us again. We want her to witness what her investments have produced and how life-changing it has been for every single one of us. Besides the beautiful Jeep, we can't wait to show her the bathrooms, the infirmary, and the study area, not to mention the improved conditions and supplies for sleeping and eating—all through the grace of God and Mother's Grace, working and loving together in a shared mission.

When Michelle and Mother's Grace arranged to have our first indoor bathroom built for us, with actual plumbing and privacy, it was as if heaven had come to our little place on Earth and we rejoiced.

Finally, we could separate any sick children away from the healthy children and provide a dose of privacy none of them had ever experienced. Later, when they expanded this to include a medical facility, we were overcome with gratitude and joy. They were saving the lives of our girls!

Of course these new additions were naturally seen as miracles for us, but for me, finding and deepening my new friendship with Michelle has become equally valuable. I know that she considers me to be special and hardworking, and I appreciate her recognition. I take care of 135 little girls now, between the ages of five and fifteen, thanks to Michelle and Mother's Grace, and it's not always so easy. But Michelle and her mission to make the world a better place have inspired *me* to do even more, however I possibly can. She is a great role model for me and teaches all of our girls what genuine compassion and empathy look like.

I will continue to fight an uphill battle in my efforts to provide safety and security for our girls. We have lost two of our children and have narrowly missed losing several more. Having a Jeep now to transport sick children is a blessing I will always be grateful for, and it helps me sleep better at night.

I am glad to be the mom of 135 angels. I see God in them every day. They are my life and create my daily happiness. No amount of gold or treasure could ever equal mothering these children as I do because the biggest satisfaction I could ever have in this world comes through the real service I provide at our orphanage. Even in times when I feel weak because there is so much to do and care for, there is always time for me to finish some things with our children.

"Lord, give me good health," I pray each day, "so that I can work for you more, and bring more souls to you."

This is my story, and I wouldn't have it any other way.

P.S. FROM MICHELLE

I will never forget my time in India with Sister Mary. She took me to places where I felt like royalty, where they welcomed me with flowers and a musical parade. Best of all, I met all of her one hundred-plus children. To this day, those were some of the happiest times I have ever had.

Sister Mary continues to inspire me to shoot for the moon. She has taught me how to create a better life from nothing. She is the culmination of true faith and real joy. She reminds me that I can do positive things even in the most difficult circumstances. If she can build buildings in tribal India while caring for 135 girls, then I'm pretty sure I can do something worthwhile in Scottsdale, Arizona, or any other place in America where I put my mind and muscle to it.

On Mother's Day last year, Sister Mary was sick with typhoid disease, which she contracted from unclean water. Even while she was so ill, she got up each morning to care for the girls in her orphanage, who numbered 185 by that time.

Remember what I've said about mothers being the backbone of the family? Sister Mary is who I'm talking about, among many others. As moms, we must rally together, inspired by each other and duty bound to support each other. *Sisterhood.* That's what organizations like Mother's Grace are all about.

Mothers need mothers.

As you read this, the new building housing Sister Mary's orphanage, complete with bathrooms, has been finished, thanks to the support of mothers like you!

#What Is Your GRACE?

TRUST

I was five years old when I witnessed my mother die in our kitchen. That day shattered my security and compromised my trust, beginning what became a lifelong habit of not trusting God to care for me, and a history of anxiety and control issues. I have always claimed to be spiritual and gone to church, and always felt that if I worked hard, then most everything would be okay. That constant push became exhausting. I never trusted that God would take care of my life, allowing me to let go, even a little bit at a time, so that I could really love and be loved.

While I was in India with Sister Mary, I went to visit Mother Teresa's house in Calcutta, a modest tribute to such an iconic figure. Being Catholic I took my time observing the relics and the entombed body of this beloved nun. I came upon a dark and desolate stairway. I felt drawn to it, in spite of a sign saying, "NO ENTRY." I snuck up the stairs toward a beautiful charcoal drawing of Mother Teresa. Suddenly I felt a gentle tap on my shoulder and jumped, thinking I had been caught and would have to report to the "head nun." Instead I was met by the most beautiful nun with the sweetest invitation, "Come with me; Jesus is waiting for you." I followed her into an illuminated room with more than thirty nuns on their knees, praying the rosary in unison. I was overcome with emotion and wept with gratitude to witness something so unearthly and beautiful.

Ever since then, any time I struggle with my faith and trust, I return to that perfect moment that will be forever etched in my soul.

Where do you go to manifest trust?

7

Lorraine Tallman:
MAKING CHEMO
COZY FOR KIDDOS

Do not wait for leaders;
do it alone, person to person.

—Mother Teresa

MEET LORRAINE TALLMAN

While scrambling one morning to get my boys out of the house and off to school, I discovered that we had no breakfast food. So we raced out the door to grab something to eat at Paradise Bakery, their favorite spot. All three ordered large muffins, large smoothies, and what seemed like an unusually large number of snacks. Ugh. Who had time to protest? As a working mom, food on the go was a godsend, and I was grateful to be able to get them fed and to school on time. As soon as the food came out, the boys immediately scarfed it all down. That's when I noticed a timid look on the cashier's face, and before she actually said the dreaded words, I knew that my credit card had been declined.

I had a lot on my plate at the time, at least metaphorically. I was recovering from chemotherapy, raising three young boys, and working full time. I could barely keep my head above water. I knew I wasn't on top of everything, but having my card declined took me by surprise. I had no cash or other cards on me, and when I saw that the boys had already eaten everything, I wondered if we could make a run for it (just kidding). I was mortified, wondering how I could get out of Paradise without making a scene.

Just as I became convinced that I was the worst role model of a parent in history, a fellow customer who saw my plight swooped in and paid the bill. This angel, Joni Di Mino, was visiting from Ohio and thinking about moving to Scottsdale. Joni and I kept in touch after I paid her back, and six months later we ran into each other, as she had relocated to the area. Then we discovered we had a mutual friend and our kids were in the same school.

Two years later, in 2012, Joni introduced me to Lorraine Tallman, whom she had met at a local gym. Knowing the work I do through Mother's Grace Foundation, Joni told me that Lorraine had lost her young daughter, Amanda, to cancer and needed help to start a 501(c)(3), which is a central part of what we do at Mother's Grace.

Lorraine and I met for coffee, and as she began to speak I felt her overwhelming sadness. She told me how she and Amanda had taken a trip to Italy before she passed away, even though Amanda wasn't considered healthy enough to go. They went anyway and Lorraine, of course, was glad they did.

During that trip, a deeply spiritual journey for mother and daughter, Lorraine promised Amanda that she would honor her daughter's final request: Give dignity back to children with cancer.

One thing about Lorraine struck me right away. Although her daughter had just passed away, Lorraine had a fire inside her that nothing could stop. On top of losing Amanda, she had an ex-husband to deal with and was struggling to pay years of medical expenses. As a single mom and a cancer survivor, I profoundly felt her pain, but I was even more moved by Lorraine's resilience and determination to turn her immense grief into a passionate campaign to honor her daughter while helping other children and their families face such familiar challenges.

I could immediately see, feel, and hear myself in Lorraine's story. As she shared her journey, I couldn't help remembering how it felt to watch my mother as a little girl and later come to realize that she would not be at my side forever. I missed the same things Lorraine and Amanda will never have—dating talks, shopping sprees, proms, weddings, close conversations, and all the highs and lows of an evolving mother/daughter relationship.

Lorraine's story was obviously heartbreaking, but I also found it beautiful because she was keen on giving grace a chance to take center stage. That's exactly what happened as we discussed plans to make it happen. The work felt effortless and natural. I learned that it's easy to forget about grace when life is okay, but its presence is illuminated when you meet a mother like Lorraine, who, in the aftermath of tragedy, became energized and ready to change the world. This remarkable mother wanted to keep her daughter's spirit alive and she knew exactly how, which she outlined to me that day in the coffee shop.

Her organization would be called Amanda Hope Rainbow Angels, and its first project would be creating Comfycozy's for Chemo—soft and warm tie-dyed shirts, with stylish and convenient openings to provide easy access for needles, tubes, and ports so that kids would no longer need to lie naked in cold hospital rooms during medical tests and treatments, such as chemotherapy. *This fun clothing would not only offer physical comfort and positive vibes; it would allow children to retain their dignity.*

Mother's Grace Foundation agreed to help and walked Lorraine through the process of setting up a nonprofit. We assisted with legal paperwork and the 501(c)(3) applications, and served as an umbrella organization and a fiduciary underwriter, which means that donations for her organization passed through our nonprofit status for the approximate six-month period it would take to get her paperwork approved.

In 2013, Amanda Hope Rainbow Angels was granted its nonprofit status and today the organization's shirts are used by hundreds of hospitals around the world. Because of one mother's grace and grit, the way children now experience chemotherapy, medical tests, and treatments has improved immensely.

Every time I check in with Lorraine, she's adding ways to help children with cancer and other life-threatening diseases. For example, she spent years convincing the international medical device company, C. R. Bard, to develop a medical-port needle device that facilitates easy, one-time access, which limits painful needle pokes and reduces anxiety and discomfort. This resulted in the invention and FDA approval of the Amanda Needle, a pain-free chemotherapy needle stabilizer made specifically for kids, which is now used in more than 200 hospitals in the U.S. and across the globe.

Grace planted the seed, Mother's Grace Foundation added the fertilizer, and Lorraine continues to water it with hard work and perseverance. No human could have possibly orchestrated the series of events that led us to Lorraine, nor could any human could go it alone while calling forth the strength to make it through the loss of a child and, in Lorraine's case, respond with an overwhelming desire to make the world a better place.

Meet the fabulous Lorraine Tallman, in her own words.

My daughter Amanda was diagnosed with leukemia when she was nine years old. She fought it for three long years, and when the doctors said she was in remission we had a celebration, a big "No More Chemo" party with lots of cake and balloons.

Three months later, Amanda came to work with me on Bring Your Child to Work Day. I'd just gotten a new job in recycle sales, for waste management. After having been out of work for nearly four years, taking care of Amanda, it was exciting for both of us. It had been a difficult few years for our family on the financial front because, when the market fell, my husband, Marty, lost his bank job for eight months, and with both of us out of work, we faced a lot of stress. Between having a child diagnosed with cancer and fearing the prospect of losing our house, we were worried all the time and it was taking a toll on everyone.

But on that day, happy to have my child healthy again and a workplace to bring her to, I felt hopeful. Amanda seemed to be enjoying herself doing crafts, but after lunch she complained about a headache.

"I don't feel good," she said.

Oh God.

My heart sank. We left work and went straight to the pediatrician.

"Lorraine, it's just a normal headache," the doctor assured me.

"Normal?"

"Yes, she's fine."

I remember driving home and thinking, *Is this what it's like to be a normal mom?*

For the last few years, nothing resembled normal. Since Amanda began treatment, normal became waking up to Amanda's pillow covered in blood. The first time this happened, I learned it was because her platelets had dropped, which is a common thing during chemo. Low platelet levels cause bleeding through the nose, eye ducts, ears, and teeth, and can even force the blood to surface up through the skin.

For a child, this really messes up their chemistry, especially because it's not even fully formed yet, so it's very destructive. That's why so many kids with cancer have liver issues and strokes because of the steroids they have to take. All childhood cancer survivors have serious long-term issues. Many end up with learning disabilities or lose part of their sight or hearing.

I was always afraid of that.

When I found Amanda that morning, still asleep, I scooped her into my arms. She woke up, looked over at the pillow, and was like, "What *is* that?"

"Oh, sorry honey, I spilled my coffee," I said, interrupting her with whatever popped into my head, anything to change the subject.

At that point, the stain had turned brown and I didn't want her to worry. She'd been bleeding for hours. It was a slow leak, while the last time the blood had been literally pouring out of her nose. I grabbed her favorite binky, which we never went to the hospital without, and flew down to the Emergency Room (ER).

"Oh, that's nothing," they said.

They had these deadpan expressions, totally unfazed.

I was like, "What?"

"Well, her platelets are low," the doctor said.

"I should have been informed about this possibility," I said.

By that point, I was in complete shock.

"Well, we usually catch it before it gets this low."

Well, clearly not.

That became the first of many highly dramatic, heart-pounding, 100 mile-an-hour races to the ER. Our new normal became eighteen months of combined days and nights at the hospital. Because Amanda didn't have any white cells, every time she got a fever, she'd have to check into the hospital for a ten-day round of IV antibiotics. While the protocols have subsequently changed since then, when Amanda was going through it, her ANC (white blood count and neutrophils) had to be at least 750 for a hospital release. That meant she could be in the hospital for ten days or three weeks at a time. We never knew.

Then came the side effects. For example, the vincristine gave Amanda horrible seizures and the chemo was hard on her liver. A lot of children with cancer end up with transplants down the road because the chemo does so much damage to their small organs.

Nobody just "sails" through chemotherapy.

It's a beast. You throw up. You get sick. You don't feel good. There are days you can't walk and even getting to the bathroom can feel like a big accomplishment.

We existed in continual fight mode as this unrelenting struggle took over our lives. Amanda didn't want anybody to touch her without me by her side. Even if I went to the bathroom for a second and someone came to treat her, I would hear her say, "No!"

Who could ever second-guess a child in such pain?

When kids go through something like this, they don't know when another headache, nausea, or dizzy spell is going to come. Every day presents a new set of challenges with insecurities and fears. My presence provided Amanda with the trust and comfort that nobody would mess up.

Amanda learned to take control of her lifelines.

Of course, this took a toll on our family. We were all living on the fly, adapting each and every day. My husband was wonderfully supportive. He would sneak wine into the hospital with cheese and crackers so we could have our date night at eleven o'clock when our other kids were in bed and Amanda was asleep in her hospital room.

Our two older daughters suffered because of the financial burdens from the medical bills and were forced to give up everything they loved. Leah, Rachel, and Amanda were each two years apart in age, at nine, eleven, and thirteen. They were hugely involved, I mean, this was their baby sister. The drugs she was on (we called them Tasmanian Devil drugs) were steroids, and she had to be on them twenty-eight days in a row. They definitely affected her mind and created havoc with her temperament. But Leah and Rachel were wonderful with Amanda most of the time.

I was always on the lookout for something going wrong, wanting to head it off and get Amanda the attention she might need before whatever it was could escalate or cause her any more pain or discomfort.

Even when we were told that Amanda was cancer-free, we had plenty to deal with, like adolescent PTSD. Post-traumatic stress disorder is huge for children and even the whole family. A lot of post-cancer trauma goes unspoken because when the good news comes that the cancer is gone, the doctors tell everyone to go home and enjoy life.

There's much more to it, starting with the stress my other children endured for so long. Siblings need a voice to express their confusion because they're often ignored. They not only lose their sibling to the disease; they lose their parents, who become so pre-occupied with everything, from bleeding to bills to praying to just making it through another day. Once you start paying for cancer treatments, the music lessons have to go, the after-school sports have to stop, and the dancing classes are finished. Not only did the girls lose all normalcy with their sibling, and then their mom; they also lost huge chunks of their own lives and far too many friendships.

They couldn't blame their sibling. They could be angry at the cancer, but where do you put those feelings? All of us had been quietly working through that process since Amanda had received a clean bill of health. But on that day, when her pediatrician said that Amanda's headache was normal, I was not reassured at all. But I pretended I was and took Amanda upstairs to rest. I reminded her that the doctor said she'd be okay.

Within 45 minutes, I heard her scream and ran to her room. The left side of Amanda's face had become completely paralyzed, and she couldn't move. I rushed her to the emergency room at Phoenix Children's Hospital, where they took her in for immediate scans on her head. Nowadays, I am a designated hand-holder to be there for moms and dads in times like this. But on that day, I could barely keep my hands from shaking, waiting for the results.

That day—exactly three months after she had been placed in remission—doctors discovered a cancerous brain mass behind her ear. Apparently, one of the leukemia treatments she had received had the potential to cause secondary cancers, but we didn't know that. We had no idea.

We sat there in shock as they told us Amanda had cancer—again.

We had to tell her, making it the worst day of our lives, only second to her passing. I couldn't do it, so we had to bring other people in to help me share this information. It's amazing that when you're a mom, the core of a family, somehow you just do what you need to do. God provides strength and courage for moments like this that you don't even know you have, but even though I always believed in God, I surely needed professional assistance in that moment.

A song I used to play, which I don't remember the name of, said, "When I'm weak, you're strong." *You better be, Amanda*, I thought, *because I'm not*. I guess I was a good pretender because that's all I could do at the time.

When you look back, you wonder how did you even do it? How were you able to function? That's one of those unspoken miracles I first learned about in church as a young girl, and I suppose my faith continued to carry me through, even to face the challenge of that day, as I sat there in that hospital, barely able to breathe.

We prepared for a bone marrow transplant, which meant a whole new regimen of chemo and radiation and finding a donor. Fortunately, one of Amanda's sisters was a perfect match, and the surgical procedure was scheduled.

That's when we found out that Amanda was dying, when we were in the hospital getting the tests done. They were putting in a second port, so Amanda was in surgery and Leah was at the cardiologist, as both departments were readying the girls for the transplant. The doctors calmly explained the science and the numbers, but they were a blur to me.

Apparently, when a particular cancer cell count is at .05 or below, meaning .05 percent of your cells or fewer have cancer in them, you are able to get a transplant. But anything higher means you can't. No chance. This was after Amanda had already been through severe radiation and chemo and we thought we were on track by bringing her cell count all the way down to make a transplant possible. They told us she was good to go, and then she wasn't. It all happened so fast.

"Lorraine, we're so sorry, but Amanda has cancer in more than 80 percent of her body. The last chemo we gave her actually mutated the cells to grow instead of going down. We can't exactly explain why this happens, but it's clear that we cannot do the transplant."

Amanda was twelve years old and wanted to be as normal as possible, to connect with her friends however she could, and just be a kid. We brought her home and chose not to tell her that she had two weeks left, that she would not live to celebrate her thirteenth birthday. She knew she didn't have the transplant but never questioned any of the medical stuff, so we just focused on the upcoming holidays.

Amanda had always wanted to see the Vatican in Rome and go on a gondola ride. It was her bucket-list thing.

"I'm believing in a miracle for you," I told her, feeling an even bigger pull into my own faith under these circumstances. "We're not going to do the transplant right now. Instead, we're going to take you to Rome to go on that gondola ride, and whatever else you want to do. We're going to have some fun."

Amanda knew that if she had the transplant, she'd be in the hospital for ten months.

My sister, who worked for American Express, asked her coworkers to pay for Amanda to live out her wish—without a tax write off—and they gave generously, raising all the money within twenty-four hours so we could buy airline tickets to go to Italy. It was just Amanda and me, her best friend and her best friend's mom, and we flew over there as soon as we could.

I grew up Catholic and my girls are strong in their faith, so this quickly became an important part of our collective experience. Each girl went through a different cycle on the journey that cancer brought us through. Sometimes they were strong; sometimes they were not.

Amanda was amazing. She said she saw a lot of angels when she was fighting cancer. I didn't see them, but she did.

"Mommy, look at those angels in the room," she'd say.

"That's nice," I'd say. "That's so sweet; that's wonderful."

When she was fighting the second time, whenever she would see angels, I would get mad and talk to God.

"Hey, get your angels out of here! You can't have her; this is enough."

Amanda was calm in these moments.

"Mom, Jesus is going to take me up to heaven; it's okay."

"It's not okay!" I'd say, but she was just so clear about everything. I knew she was going to heaven, and she knew, too. She made it more real for me. I had always believed in heaven. I always believed Jesus died on the cross. God gave me peace in my heart.

God is love, in whatever language you speak and wherever you are. If you seek Him out, and the pure love He has for you as His child, you will find it. I always tell people that God is a gentleman. He's not going to barge in on you unless you invite Him in. He may knock on the door, but unless you open it, you're not going to know Him.

With this history deep in my heart, we headed for Rome. Amanda knew God even better than I. It was just a part of her being, part of her essence.

Our doctor collaborated with the pediatric hospital in Rome, so by the time we arrived they knew all about Amanda. We paid for insurance to fly her home, in case she passed away, because there was a very real possibility that she would die on our trip.

We toured Rome in a wheelchair, and it was interesting. You don't see many wheelchairs in Italy. I don't know what they do with people who depend on them because they have cobblestone roads everywhere. People look at you like you're an idiot for bringing somebody in a wheelchair out in public. In fact, some people stared at us, as if we were doing something ridiculous to disturb them.

It became comical. I had Amanda sit on one of those elephant pet pillows, which was one of her favorite things, and she would hang on to the elephant ears as we rolled down the bumpy streets, bouncing all over the place. Getting her wheelchair in and out of those teeny, tiny taxis was virtually impossible, and on top of that we had to deal with a taxi strike that paralyzed the city. We ended up hiring people who weren't official taxi cab drivers, which meant we had to walk around the corner so they could pick us up; so we wouldn't get stuck in the middle of two loud Italians, fighting over a girl in a wheelchair.

When we booked our trip, we didn't realize that an order of nuns lived on the first two floors of the building where we were staying, and that their church was located next door. The nuns loved Amanda. They prayed for her every morning and invited us into their private quarters where millions of dollars worth of artwork was hanging in full view for anyone to see. The nuns were fabulous. They blessed Amanda and gave her little wooden crosses, which she was thrilled to hold.

It was remarkable because when we left for Italy, Amanda was often in pain, and she couldn't walk well at all. But while we were there, she became stronger and stronger every single day. We were sending pictures back to the hospital, and they were like, "Oh my God!"

Amanda got to see everything she wanted to see on that ten-day trip, from the Coliseum to the Vatican, and even Venice. We did everything, and we did it fast.

When we got home, her oncologist could hardly believe it when she walked into the office without a wheelchair in sight.

"I don't know what holy water you drank, but this is unbelievable; she's doing fantastic."

His reaction continued to give my family hope that God would do a special miracle for Amanda and that she wouldn't die. You never give up hope, and we never did.

During those next months, Amanda got to do a lot of things. She saw the baby panda in the San Diego Zoo when it was born, and the sea turtles, too, which she loved, and she even swam with dolphins. Seeing her manage everything she ever wanted to do was beautiful, exquisite beyond words. How many people get to say they have done everything they ever wanted to do in life, like their entire bucket list?

Amanda's last eight days were spent in an amazing hospice facility, the Ryan House in Phoenix. We created a galaxy of stars on the ceiling of her room, and they had a pool, a movie theater room, and a beautiful kitchen. She loved it and asked why we hadn't brought her to this place before because it was so happy there.

"I don't know, sweet girl," I said. "But I'm glad it's a happy place for you now."

Family flew in from New York, Michigan, Pennsylvania, and Albuquerque, so that Amanda could spend her last days totally surrounded by people who knew and loved her. The Ryan House was so accommodating and even let our family sleep there. Each night, when we gathered in the kitchen to prepare a meal, we fed anyone else who was staying at the Ryan House or had friends and family visiting because that's just the Italian thing to do.

Amanda fought for nine months until she passed away, two weeks before her thirteenth birthday.

It was a remarkable time even though I hardly remember it.

I do remember laying on top of her in her hospice bed, nose to nose, telling her it was okay to go to heaven, that she could go be with Jesus now. When she took her last breath, she almost had this little smile on her mouth. I was looking at her, sobbing, and I was thinking and speaking to God. "Okay, you took Lazarus up in three days if you want to bring her back right now, that's the miracle we want."

I actually thought that in that moment: *Like okay, you can bring her back now if that's what you need for this story, for this testimony of yours. Bring her back.* Of course, He didn't.

Later that year, a friend of mine, Joni Di Mino, introduced me to Michelle, who had founded the Mother's Grace Foundation. It was the first time since the whole thing began with Amanda's first diagnosis that I met another mother who had been through something like me.

Up until that time, I had been existing in such a lonely place. I had lost friends I thought I would never lose. It's hard to text people and keep them up to date on what's happening because you just don't want to talk about it more than you absolutely have to, and people don't always get that, no matter how well-meaning they are. It's always bad news, no matter how you spin it, so I didn't want to repeat any of it out loud.

Besides, I needed to process things for myself. My husband and I shared things on Facebook, but I wasn't in a place to make fifty phone calls a day and repeat the same information over and over again. Unfortunately, some people were offended when we didn't return their calls or text them back, but we didn't want to continually talk about it. We couldn't!

Amanda's cancer, and all that came with it, had overtaken our lives, and in what little spare time there was, I needed a break. I needed silence and solace and peace, and that can never exist in a whirlwind of phone calls and texting and reporting the latest news.

On that Friday night, when the rest of the world just stopped, I was drinking and walking around our front yard, pacing, as if continually moving might change the facts. The house was filled with neighbors and all of our family had flown in. This was the day she passed. Amanda had been in hospice for eight days, and I think we had more visitors than the hospice had ever seen in their history. There were at least forty family members there every day, flying in and out, cooking meals and feeding the whole place.

Amanda was still seeing angels throughout this entire process, even in hospice.

"Mom, Jesus is going to heal me, or I'm going to heaven. It's okay."

Our pastor from church came over that Friday night. He had never been in the hospice, so he didn't know what the room looked like.

"I had a vision this morning," he said, and the time corresponded exactly to when Amanda had passed away. "God got up from the throne room and came down and took Amanda. It looked like you were lying on her in a room filled with stars and there were people as far as I could see. God came down and swooped her from underneath you and He said, 'It's okay, I've got her from here,' and He spun her around and she smiled at me, and they went up to heaven."

I had just been yelling at Jesus in that exact moment, and I remember saying, "If You send Your goddamn angels to take my daughter, I'll never talk to You again. If you want her You better come off that throne and get her Yourself."

I actually said that out loud, and then the pastor came that night and told me that story because I was so mad at the angels. That brought me peace and understanding, to know that God came and had her. He was going to take care of her, and I was going to keep my promises to her.

This brings me to Amanda's desire to help children with cancer. Even though she was only twelve, she saw things crystal clear. Being sick is an education in itself when you realize that the world is not all doughnuts and Disney.

She had seen several friends in the hospital who were dying. All the children there hear the nurses, even when they are discreet, because the comments are not always whispered. Children also see the faces of other families and they notice how broken many of them are. When they go to the playroom and a friend they've known for years is no longer there, what do they think? *Is it my turn next?*

Amanda was wise beyond her years. I've often said my daughter lived more life in twelve years than some people do in sixty or more. I think she knew, even though we never came out and said, "You're dying," she definitely knew. She saw heaven. She had no fear of where she was going. She just knew she was going to get healed or she was going to go to heaven.

"Whatever happens," she'd say. "I'm good."

It was freaky. None of this recall gave me any peace until after the pastor came to our home and shared his story. Amanda was not alone, and never will be.

She made me keep our promise.

"Mommy, look at me with both eyes. Are you listening with both ears? You need to promise me that you will help every child fighting cancer. Not everyone has a mama like you."

"Don't use my words against me!" I said, referring to the wishes I had expressed to her before, that no child should ever have to go through anything like this.

"Mama, promise."

I promised. I wasted no time in creating Amanda Hope Rainbow Angels. I've always had business development know-how and product development is in my blood, so the challenge of starting a new business was not terribly daunting. Have you ever seen those single-wrapped roses in convenience stores with the teddy bears? I started that business in the 1980s and I owned it for twenty years. It was called Roseworld.

But a nonprofit was another story. I had a lot to learn. That's when a burst of grace and serendipity led me to meeting Michelle and becoming part of Mother's Grace.

Michelle and I fell in love with each other right from the start. Not only was she going through her own cancer at the time, but her son was ill, too, with juvenile diabetes, which is a dangerous thing for sure. She understood me, not only the hurt I was feeling from seeing Amanda go through chemotherapy, but the extreme anxiety and fear that never goes away from seeing your child in pain and not being able to do anything about it.

Both of us had experienced that unbelievable level of frustration and disappointment, the feeling that, "Shit, something has got to be done because how ridiculous it is for people to suffer like this, anyone, but especially your own child."

Luckily, I have a few friends like Michelle, and you only need a few good ones to get by. I refer to them as my journey walkers, the genuine friends who can fight the fight and walk the walk as they go deep on the journey with you.

We have to hold one another's hands because life is hard. Sometimes we're too busy to even notice how hard it is. But it is. It's hard. It's very hard. You have to keep picking yourself up, and it's the people that you pick yourself up with that get you through it.

Michelle and I are both on a mission to help families and not everybody understands us. Sometimes we're too passionate or opinionated. But it's the passion that connects us and brings us to the other side of trauma, wherever that leads us.

Dealing with trauma and tragedy has given me the empathy and compassion I need to feel love and patience for others, but it's not going to rule me. This entire saga of loss and pain and suffering has brought me to a different place. Part of my belief is that we can take our experience into the future, that horrible things happen, and we may never let go unless we work at it. But we can take those experiences and turn them into good if we can really look at them and ask how we can help someone else through a similar experience. I think that process takes the evil and softens it a little bit. It's like, "I'm not going to let that evil thing that happened to me take my life from me. I'm going to make something good of it."

Michelle and Mother's Grace helped me fund the $2,500 I needed for the 501(c)(3). At that time, my husband and I went through complete financial devastation. But Amanda told me that she wanted every child to get a Comfycozy for Chemo adapted apparel she had first imagined.

Amanda died March 30, 2012. We helped our first 600 children in December 2012, before our official nonprofit was even totally set up. I didn't wait. I couldn't. I put my loss and grief right to work. Amanda had designed this Comfycozy apparel line, and it took me a while to find a manufacturer and learn how to do it, what it would actually look like, and how it would function. People in the community who had known Amanda wanted to help. I was committed full time to this right from the start, from the moment she passed away. I couldn't go back to work. My mind could not wrap around any of that. All of my energy and passion has been about perpetuating Amanda's legacy.

Lots of people advised me to take a couple of years off after Amanda's death to grieve, but I was having none of it. I was on a mission, and it was quite simple, really, at least in my mind.

"No. It was my daughter's last dying wish," I told people, "and I'm not going to sit on it for two years, or anything like that. That would mean fewer kids would get help, and I'm not going to be the one not to help them."

Keeping my promise to Amanda has never been in question.

My drive was also fueled by my anger at the pediatric cancer world for not doing better. People wonder how I'm doing, and the simple truth is, I'm a pissed-off mom. We went through all of this, and it shouldn't have been this way. Do I have great faith in God? Yes. But I am angry. For instance, why are we still using the same drugs we developed in 1950 when we know they give cancer a second chance? Why on earth are they being used to this day?

As much as my goal is to bring dignity and modesty and family-centered care and education to Americans because that's what this journey is all about, it's also about me being really mad at the world for allowing this to continue. I could scream like a crazy person, but what is that going to do? My promise to Amanda was to help every child and family, and while anger may sometimes give me energy, I can't let it rule my psyche.

I go into hospitals and hold moms' hands. I'm the mom that hospitals call to tell me a mother is about to lose her child. That's when I show up, no questions asked. God gives me the strength of words in that moment for the special mom, and dad, too, of course. It's not my background but for some reason, I find words of encouragement. You have to have some sort of empathy for it to be a soulful connection. It helps when a parent looks into my eyes and knows that I know. I deeply appreciate those moments because I'm the take-a-deep-breath person. That's me. It's nothing I need to say. When someone is going through hell and back, like a hurricane that happens randomly without any preparation, you may think you're good, but then you're not, and you need someone who knows the territory.

You have to reinvent yourself. A new you definitely emerges. I am not the same woman I once was. I'm new, even from a week ago. I go through these experiences with families I connect with, and I have different conversations with moms and dads and siblings, depending on their personalities and backgrounds.

One dad I met was not doing well, and I remember just grabbing him and holding him firmly. He was a successful CEO, but nothing can prepare you for seeing your child in such pain.

"Breathe," I told him. "That's all you need to do today. Breathe."

I'm a huge proponent of family-centered care. The whole family needs to be in on decisions, and doctors need to take care of the whole family. That's why we opened a free counseling service *without* insurance issues. People come to us and get free help whenever they want, simply because of what my family went through; we needed counseling so badly but couldn't afford it. Now, that's changed, at least for all the families we can service.

It's not just the kids with cancer, either. There are so many siblings that walk through our door that are suicidal. It's mind-boggling. Those kids aren't getting the normal range of attention from their parents; they're not even getting a normal dose, so they start doing anything to get attention, and those are often unhealthy things, depending on their age.

It is said that the pathway to hell is filled with good intentions. You can *mean* to do something, but it's meaningless until you really *do* it. So why do people sometimes fall short of actualizing their intentions? A fear of not succeeding is what holds many people back.

I was determined not to let myself become one of those people. I was going to fulfill my promise to Amanda, no matter what. I knew that something had to be done, and that I was the only one to see it through.

For the previous three years, I had seen the lack of available resources and a shortage of appropriate help in the world of pediatrics. People who have experienced life and loss are much more motivated to make a difference in the world than those who have never been there. We now provide many needed services, but one of the most important things we do is create what I call "major distractions." This comes from a central idea of wanting children who fight cancer to have happy memories along their journey. Unlike adult cancer treatments, which can typically last from three weeks to six months, pediatric cancer can take two to five years to treat.

We give these children and their families something to look forward to and we do our best to create happy moments they can look back on, to provide hope and faith in the future.

I also get to advocate for patient-centered care, which is essentially what Amanda demanded during her second round with cancer. Imagine a twelve-year-old telling you that you can't just walk in and start poking her with needles and not even know her name. That was Amanda, at her best, teaching her medical team a better, more humane way to be.

I appear at conferences and as a speaker/educator for the Phoenix Children's Hospital Family Advisory Council. I talk to new interns, nurses, and other new hires about my story, about family-centered care, and how to be a better provider.

I often hear, "You've made me a better doctor. I never thought of it that way. Thank you for sharing your story."

I love that. It makes my work worthwhile.

Sometimes, when I talk about Amanda, I cry. It's a part of my life and part of my healing, and I'm okay with it. This experience has also taught me about faith and grace. Now I have the faith to know that I will lead people in the right direction because it happens all the time. I live a grace-filled life, and I know it, and I wouldn't have it any other way.

Nearly three years ago—six years after Amanda passed—my husband, Marty, was diagnosed with a rare form of stomach cancer, making it our third cancer fight together. We were determined to kick cancer's ass, and we used everything we had learned during our experience with Amanda. For example, on chemo days we watched funny videos and traded stories. Once again, it was time to take many deep breaths and to call on my journey walkers, who never failed to be there for me. But even my best supporters could not perform a miracle, and Marty passed away two years ago, after a much-too-short losing battle with this disease.

Sometimes there are no answers to the questions I have, but I just need someone to listen anyway, as it's too much sometimes to feel alone when dealing with this kind of loss.

This is especially true during the Christmas season because Amanda was a Christmas fanatic. For her, we never had enough lights and she wanted five Christmas trees instead of one. She was just a crazy Christmas girl. After she passed, it was never easy, and since Marty died, it's been even more difficult. But my daughters and I carry on with open hearts.

A year after she died, Amanda's dog got hit by a car. My daughters had a unique and extremely healthy reaction. "Oh, Amanda's such a spoiled, rotten brat; she wanted her dog in heaven with her."

When we lost Marty, who was so close with them, they responded in a similar way. "Mom, so help me God," they told me, "she better not take anyone else. If Amanda tries to take you to heaven, too, we're going to kill her."

So that's how they're dealing with it. That dose of humor is really necessary and fundamental, and that's also something we touch on in our treatment paradigm because that's rarely included anywhere else. There's too much tiptoeing around.

My mission remains to fulfill the promise I made to my daughter. I can never let this world forget that Amanda was alive. It's not going to happen. It gets me out of bed every morning, when I see what God has for me that day.

We've literally helped thousands of children all over the world, in China and Ireland and England and Guam and Venezuela. We have a pipeline of projects ready to go as soon as we secure the funds and time to make them happen, and we will!

We've become partners with Bard Access Systems, a medical equipment design and supply company, to create a special stabilizer for inserting IV needles into chemo ports, called the Amanda Needle. The FDA legal name is the Amanda Port Stabilizer. This came about because every time Amanda needed to have her port accessed, the ER nurses, not specially trained oncology nurses, had a one-inch or an inch-and-a-half needle that they stuck into the port in her chest, but they would often miss. Amanda would be in such pain whenever this happened. After watching the nurse miss the insertion three times on one occasion, and seven times another night, I knew I had to do something.

"Stop hurting me!"

I couldn't bear to hear Amanda or any other child screaming this any longer, and none of them should ever have to endure such a thing. I reached out to the president of the company.

"Why can't you find a better way? Why is it so hard for your ports to be accessed? Why does my daughter have to be tortured every time she goes to the emergency room?"

They were not aware that this was an issue. HIPPA laws, meant to support patient privacy, don't allow manufacturers to gather feedback from patients, and the ER nurses weren't the ones to get through. The problem is, emergency room nurses are not trained to access a port, which is the protocol when a patient enters the ER. They don't get to oncology until they're admitted, and you can't get admitted until the port is accessed in the ER. Even though Bard was conducting research with providers, they weren't talking to the patients or ER nurses at the level where the nightmares were happening. Kids were taking Benadryl and Ativan to keep them calm because the nurses knew they would miss the targets. They knew they would hurt them, and they hated doing that, but they simply weren't trained to do any better, especially with a child. This was a vicious cycle because every time Amanda needed to be admitted as an inpatient, we had to go through the ER system. With children with cancer, most of the time they're there because their blood levels drop so low, they have no white blood cells, and you can't have a child in that condition walking down the street. They have to be admitted. It was horrible.

We had to initiate change ourselves, and that's exactly what I did by reaching out to Bard. They flew me to Utah where I met with thirty engineers. I told them my story in full detail, and by the time I finished, they were sobbing.

"Lorraine, we're going to fix this."

For the next couple of years, I met with the engineers doing 3D printing to figure out how it could work and how to make it. It took a long time. Then it went to the FDA, and holy moly, those people took forever. Like, get a real life, please. This is plastic; we're not talking about a drug; this is a guidance system for a needle. It's not rocket science. It may not appear like a tricky thing, but every phase required taking the prototype to a nursing and oncology conference, and having a hundred nurses test it out. A lot of research goes into every detail because you can't develop something and have nurses say they don't want to use it. You need to get them to be a part of the process. They really need to know that this product will make their life easier, which the Amanda Needle does. Now that it's been approved and manufactured, it's going through hospital politics to get them to spend the extra money for the stabilizer, and that's a whole other challenge we're working on. I'll be visiting a lot of hospitals to tell Amanda's story and make my pitch.

I never question why I have chosen to do this with my life or if I am capable. I was a normal suburban mom, full of pain, exhaustion, and dealing with a lack of finances, and I turned all of that loss and grief into something positive because why not? What a waste of a life to not even try.

Not only did I make a promise to Amanda, I feel an obligation to be a steady and positive role model for my two daughters. My mission means more than that, too, as it's become my own path to tranquility and light.

I've been told that our tears are treasures in heaven, and if that's true, there must be a river with my name on it. No matter how tough someone looks on the outside, we're all fragile. I'm grateful that people continue to be there for me during times like this, and I want to be part of someone else's fragile moment, too. Like minds think alike, and like hearts feel the same way.

Spend your life with a grateful heart because tomorrow is never promised. If that's the only thing I can offer you, I think it's worth a look.

P.S. FROM MICHELLE

Lorraine is vulnerable, humble, and human, and on the day we met, she invited us both to heal. Like the other moms in this book, Lorraine is a regular gal, a mom who reacted to personal tragedy by choosing to improve the lives of others.

We helped Lorraine, but the reality is, she helped me much more. After my mom died, and when I had cancer, I became stuck in a cycle of torment. At times, the fear paralyzed me, but Lorraine, faced with her own burdens, didn't waste a moment wrapped up in her own pain. Instead of collapsing, she took action. Her pain was not any less—I felt it in her eyes and in her voice the first time we met—but she allowed the wound to lead her.

Lorraine is my friend for life. I don't believe in accidents. She was meant to enter my life, and to this day I am grateful she did.

#What Is Your **GRACE?**

LOVE

The night before I began chemotherapy in 2008, I took my seven-year-old son to the doctor, as he was feeling out of sorts and not looking well. I attributed this to my health crisis, but I wanted to be sure. Within five minutes, he was diagnosed with juvenile diabetes. This ridiculous shock seemed unbearable as I was already dealing with cancer. He spent five days in the hospital and I began my chemotherapy. Thank God for our extended family.

We learned as much as we could about diabetes. Halfway into my treatment, just after celebrating our twentieth wedding anniversary, my husband told me he was unsure of his feelings for me and our marriage. What else could I possibly be asked to deal with on top of diabetes and cancer? It was insane. I suffered incredible anxiety that I would be alone with all this stress, and even worse, that no one would be around to love me after I got through my treatment.

Prior to this, I had worked my way up to a VP position in a Fortune 500 company, gaining much respect in a male-dominated industry. I had three beautiful and healthy boys. I was ready for my close-up, with my career, marriage, family, friends, and community all in place.

When all of this hit, I was stripped of my happy little

reality. I hated the way I looked and felt. I had no hair. My body felt crumpled and broken. I lost thirty pounds I didn't need to lose. On top of that, we had severe financial issues, which caused constant panic.

During all that time, the one thing I never did was lose faith. I prayed every day and cried out to God for support and direction. I wrote about it, talked about it, looked for signs, listened to others on the subject, and reached out for love. That's what carried me—love.

How does love carry you?

8

Kristen Salcito Sandquist and Jennifer Noelani Spenser: EMPOWERING DREAMS BEYOND DISABILITY

What does it take to be the first female anything?
It takes grit, and it takes grace.

—Meryl Streep

MEET KRISTEN SALCITO SANDQUIST AND JENNIFER NOELANI SPENSER

One Sunday after Mass, nearly nine years ago, my three boys and I headed out for sushi, as we often used to do after Sunday service. As we sat outside in the beautiful Arizona weather and chatted away like usual, I saw a similar family next to us and one of the boys was wearing a T-shirt from the same Catholic school my boys attended.

I felt some cosmic energy toward the mom and we soon found out that each of us had been eavesdropping on each other's conversation as we munched on sashimi. Turns out we both had the same idea: this woman needs to become my friend!

For some odd yet divine reason, two total strangers began chatting that day and immediately clicked so intensely that our boys left us to our chatter while they headed home. Right then and there, over glasses of green tea, we dropped right into what became the start of a long and wonderful friendship, based on nothing special and something very special, too. We both were in our early years of starting charitable organizations— Mother's Grace and Kristen's K2 Adventures Foundation.

As Kristen explained, in 2009, Kevin Cherilla led eight blind individuals in a rigorous climb up Mt. Kilimanjaro. Among his guides was mother and athlete, Kristen Sandquist. During this historic climb, every member of the team made the summit—and four world records were broken. The experience was so powerful that Kevin and Kristen co-founded K2 Adventures, a foundation and travel company that infuses potential where others see limitations and now provides children and adults with disabilities (and their families) the means to hike mountains like Kilimanjaro and other seemingly unattainable feats.

I was so intrigued by her story, as it had been a dream of mine to go to Africa. Kristen and her partner, Kevin, co-founded K2 with a mission to offer uniquely qualified guides to lead people with special challenges on international expeditions. K2 assists military veterans, amputees, and visually impaired individuals in their quest to conquer mountains and build a new understanding of what is possible.

Africa, hiking, volunteering—all up my alley and all exciting, and Kristen was so bright and full of positive energy. We continued our conversation in the coming weeks and months and began to team up on projects we co-sponsored with several moms who had disabled children and needed specially equipped vans.

As my life always seems to unfold, divine things began to happen.

I mentioned to a dear friend this opportunity to volunteer in Africa with K2 and she already knew all about them and had discussed a trip that included hiking Mt. Kilimanjaro. I wanted to volunteer, and she wanted to hike the entire mountain. I had never even considered doing anything like that, but as we discussed it over the next year, I became intrigued.

On my fiftieth birthday, July 22, 2015, my friend, Angela, and I, along with five of our six boys, my sixty-five-year-old uncle, and highly skilled members of K2 Adventures Travel, I summited Kilimanjaro—all the way to the top—with my own two feet. This cemented an already beautiful connection with Kristen and led to a new kinship with Jennifer Noelani Spenser.

During May 2017, while traveling for business, I was scrambling through Seattle traffic on my way to a meeting when a call came from an old friend back home, Sheila Doherty. Normally, I would let it go straight to voice mail and return it on the weekend, but for some reason I picked up and heard a distraught Sheila on the other end.

Jenn Spenser, a long time committee member with Mother's Grace, needed help. She had reached out to Sheila, among others, regarding her son, Kainoa, who had just come home from college with a life-threatening, flesh-eating bacteria and was failing fast. They were at a small local hospital, hoping we might have a connection at the Mayo Clinic in Phoenix because he needed immediate attention from an infectious disease specialist. I immediately contacted the Mother's Grace board, and by a stroke of divine providence, one of our members, Angela Ducey, got the CEO of Mayo on the phone and they sent a team of doctors to evaluate the situation. Within an hour, they had Kainoa on bypass and ready for transport to Mayo.

What happened in the next days, weeks, and months can best be told by Jenn, but after months in the hospital, we arranged temporary housing for Kainoa and his family until we could get them in a home that was Americans with Disabilities Act (ADA) compliant and user friendly for the overwhelming physical challenges he would be facing. At that time, I called Kristen to tell her about Kainoa and brought her and Kevin to visit him at their temporary housing.

Ever since that day, Kainoa has been working with K2, trailblazing the way with great plans and an inspirational message for those with disabilities who want to forge forward with their lives. It's a marriage meant to be, a story that has come full circle in amazing grace.

Kristen, Kevin, and I continue to partner on all levels to provide support and avenues for success for those overcoming physical challenges. I continue to hike with them, and Angela and I are always planning our next big adventure. Everest Base Camp, here we come.

Jenn Spenser continues her great work with the Mother's Grace family and works with physicians and medical device manufacturers to elevate prosthetic awareness and support, as well as provide guidance to families who have no idea how to navigate this difficult territory.

Even though he lost all four of his limbs, which his doctors at the Mayo Clinic proclaimed a miracle recovery, Kainoa now works in the Governor's office, arranged by the inimitable Angela Ducey.

There is nothing these two women can't do and I am thrilled to share the stories of Kristen Salcito Sandquist and Jennifer Noelani Spenser, in their own words.

KRISTEN

I found something I love when Kevin Cherilla and I created K2 Adventures Foundation and K2 Adventure Travel. Kevin and Kristen—K2. It all clicked. I saw a giant opportunity right from the start to create an organization that could inspire people to improve their physical, mental, and spiritual health as they came to realize the limitless potential of the human spirit.

That's exactly what I tell my kids: find something you love and run with it! You want to go to work each day and genuinely enjoy what you're doing, so you can go to bed at night and say, "Today was a good day. I did something new and the world can be a better place because of my efforts." If you can say this to yourself each night, then you're doing the right job.

After graduating from Arizona State University, I got married and went to work as an eighth-grade teacher in Sheboygan, Wisconsin. Many of my students came from abusive homes and struggled with a lack of food and clothes. I started my first nonprofit organization, called Circle of Friends, and got two corporate sponsors to help me reach my goal of providing students with an opportunity to get the winter clothes and food they badly needed. What started in one school ended up serving twenty-six schools over the next twenty-five years.

Circle of Friends launched me into my second nonprofit, Visions of Hope, which I started when I came back to Arizona in 2009. I took a different approach this time and partnered with other local non-profits to serve a greater population. This opened up opportunities to work with the disability community. During a charity event I was hosting, a man walked up to me and said, "I know a guy who's going to take eight blind climbers to Tanzania, Africa, to climb Mount Kilimanjaro. I think you two should meet."

A couple days later, I met Kevin Cherilla, a mountain climber who worked with individuals in the disability world on hiking and outdoor recreational activities. He had a ton of experience in his world and I had plenty in mine. We started talking.

"Can you help me raise money for this blind team I want to guide on Mount Kilimanjaro? Each member has to raise funds in order to be a part of the team," he asked.

"I'd love to help you with that. Why don't we host a fundraiser? We could take the money we raise and donate it back to the Foundation for Blind Children, which would let them use it to take those kids on the trip," I said.

"Do you have any desire to climb Mount Kilimanjaro?" Kevin asked.

That gave me pause.

"I've never slept outside. I've certainly never peed outside, either, or even been in a tent. I'm not a camping person, as you can see, but I'm intrigued. I love the outdoors and the idea of working with a person who's blind, but I'm not really sure this is my gig."

Kevin patiently explained the essence of the trip.

"Climbing Mount Kilimanjaro isn't the highlight. Meeting the people and serving in the orphanage there is what's going to change your life because that's who you are. Come with us as a guide to help and see what you think when you get there."

"Okay, I'm in."

I went home, excited to tell the news to my husband. "Honey, I met this great guy today who is really nice and he's taking a team of eight blind individuals to climb Mount Kilimanjaro and he asked me to be a guide and I said yes."

My husband looked at me calmly. "Do you even know where Kilimanjaro is?"

"Not really."

"Kristen, I totally support this, but you've never hiked a day in your life; and you're leaving in fifty-something days; you're going to guide a woman who's blind; and you've never slept outside. I mean, you've never done anything outside the United States."

"Well, I think it will be fun."

"Read about it."

"No, no, if I read about it, I might not do it, and I already committed to the team."

I bought my gear and called Kevin.

"I'm in. I'm doing this, so I need to train. You better teach me how to hike."

I was a real project. I needed to get in shape and conditioned for high altitude. I met with a trainer named Kelly, and told her my situation. I trained and trained and trained, working on my own and with Cindy and Tanner, the two blind individuals I'd be guiding on the mountain. I knew that I would be guiding them every day, so I learned to *bell guide*, *backpack guide*, and *bar guide*, all techniques for leading individuals who are blind. I loved the process and couldn't wait to go.

When we arrived in Tanzania, Africa, we went straight to the Mwereni Integrated School of the Blind and Disabled. As soon as we walked in the door, my life changed forever.

"Kevin, I can't leave here and not see every day what I have just seen. I want to do more. I *need* to do more. I have to. I don't know what that looks like and I don't know what that means, but I want to do more."

What first impacted me was meeting a young boy named Sadie, who was blind and had xeroderma pigmentosum (XP). This is a rare genetic condition characterized by, among other things, a severe sensitivity to ultraviolet rays. In Tanzania to be born blind or with XP is culturally unacceptable. Most individuals are shunned by their families or given up to an orphanage, if they are not terminated at birth or sold for witchcraft. In this orphanage, all the orphans are either albino, suffering with XP, or blind.

Sadie came up to me and held my hand.

"Lady," he said, which was all he had to do to win my heart.

He was ten, the same age as my son back home.

Sadie held my hand everywhere we went and kept calling out one word.

"Lady, lady, lady," as if I was the mother he was missing.

I had a bracelet on my wrist.

"Sadie, do you like my bracelet?"

"I love your bracelet."

"Do you want my bracelet?"

"I *do* want your bracelet. I'll remember you forever."

I took it off and I put it on Sadie's little wrist.

"Are you going to keep my bracelet so when I come back next year I get to see it again?"

"Are you going to come back?"

"I'm definitely coming back."

I knew I wasn't making that up, that I was already locked into a new phase in my life, beginning right then and there in this orphanage in Africa. I wasn't just telling him what he wanted to hear. I knew—no question about it. I took Sadie's hand and we walked into his bedroom, which he shared with six other kids, sleeping on four beds. His mattress was in pretty bad shape and he didn't have a pillow or a blanket.

"I love your bedroom, Sadie; I think it's beautiful."

He picked up his mattress to put the bracelet underneath it, and I saw a crowbar stashed there, which kind of stunned me.

"Sadie, what is that under your mattress?"

"It's for protection."

Once again, I knew that my life was changed forever.

This government orphanage held twenty-four children who didn't have enough food, clothing, or basic necessities. The government provided minimal funds, just enough for the kids to survive.

There was a school attached to the orphanage with 500 "regular" kids and the orphans were mainstreamed with little to no special care. The school was at the bottom of the totem pole, ranked last in the country in academics and testing scores. Luckily, the other kids didn't harm Sadie or his friends, as the stigmas they suffer from are much more of an adult invention.

That was ten years ago.

I was overwhelmed, and I hadn't yet gone near the mountain.

Kevin and the team had arranged for Braille writers, magnifiers, and canes to be shipped from the States, all donated, which was incredible. I managed to collect myself and gear up for the mountain: hiking every single day, guiding one or two people at a time, and sleeping and peeing outside for the first time in my life!

All the while, even as we climbed, Kevin and I were hatching a business plan for what became K2 Adventures Foundation and K2 Adventure Travel.

The entire team made the summit with 100 percent success. Eight blind climbers, sixteen sighted guides, and our expedition leader. We took a ton of photos and celebrated breaking four world records for doing such a climb with this diverse group.

A week after returning home, Kevin and I discussed starting an international nonprofit. K2 Adventures Foundation opened three months later as a fully operational international nonprofit organization. During that time, we also built and created K2 Adventure Travel, which launched just months later. The theory behind that was to take individuals who want to do a bucket list item and immerse them into the local culture, just like what happened to me, and to offer them an opportunity to give back. People who just donate to the foundation can do that, and the money goes toward individuals with disabilities. People who want to climb with us do community service before they do the mountain.

Plenty of groups take people on mountain hikes and expeditions, and philanthropy organizations are bountiful, but no company mixes the two like we do, especially with our two separate companies that complement each other. Climb Kilimanjaro and become a better person. Learn more about other cultures. It's never just about the mountain. It's about affecting people's lives.

K2 Adventures Foundation is our qualified 501(c)(3), an IRS-regulated nonprofit. We're running really smoothly now. We did about $1.3 million this year, and we're giving back about 80 to 90 cents on the dollar, which makes us proud. Our office is in Scottsdale, Arizona. We have six people working with the foundation on a daily basis, and four people assigned to the travel company. Kevin and I volley back and forth.

Our foundation's mission is to serve individuals with disabilities in the United States and around the world. We offer awards to individuals to help them go above and beyond their disability and get properly educated and equipped. In a sense, we provide advanced physical therapy, things insurance companies deny because they consider them luxury items. We don't believe that an adaptive piece of equipment or an adaptive running blade for a loss of limb is a luxury item. If you are a person who lost both legs, we want to help you get adaptive legs to go out and hike.

The worst thing you can tell someone is "You're not qualified or able to try." How sad is it for somebody else to determine your fate? How about saying something different, like, "I don't care what it takes. Let's figure it out." That's us. We are constantly asking how we can make sure that disability does not carry a stigma with it.

It's not disability; it's ability.

Our global programs are in Tanzania, Peru, and Nepal, and we work with individuals in those countries who are facing adversity. We take people to fulfill their bucket list items, to climb Mount Kilimanjaro, to see Machu Picchu, and to trek to the Mount Everest base camp. When you're on those trips, we take you to an orphanage or a hospital where you can serve individuals who really need you. After you travel, your heart will be touched, and you will likely make a donation to our foundation. If you start as a travel client, you will want to stay involved.

"Wow, I climbed Mount Kilimanjaro, but that wasn't what made my entire trip. I went to an orphanage and saw kids who are blind and lost their limbs, who live in fear because their government doesn't support them. This organization guided me to the top of Mount Kilimanjaro and they're giving back to these individuals. I want to give back to these individuals, too."

This is a typical response.

I've done Kilimanjaro eighteen times. Kevin has done it thirty-nine times, and in ten years we've taken more than 1,500 people with us. When we're in a tent at night, our conversations always go back to the first two days of the trip. What better place to meditate on that than when you're climbing?

For me, that meant everything the first time, when I met Sadie, climbed Kilimanjaro, and came home to start K2 with my intrepid partner, Kevin.

I saw Sadie the next year when we returned to Tanzania. I saw him every year we visited until he passed away last year. We were there near the end when he was so sick with the xeroderma pigmentosum, which took his life. One month before he died, Sadie sang a song to me. This was one of the hardest things I've ever been through because this young man was so instrumental in my personal transformation and in the development and growth of our company.

Kevin and I covered all the funeral expenses and the celebration of life for his family. He ended up going home to his father and mother just before he passed away. His family actually loved him and cared about him. But they didn't want him living in the community because they were afraid something bad would happen to him. They knew that he would be safe in that orphanage. His family visited him sometimes, which was rare.

Since we first visited the orphanage, we have contributed about $3.5 million in aid and assistance. The whole compound is completely sustainable at this point, including newly built chicken coops, an eight-acre garden, classrooms, a kitchen, laundry, medical clinic, and a dental clinic. We brought a tractor for the gardening and employed many individuals to keep it flourishing. The Mwereni Integrated

School of the Blind and Disabled now houses seventy-five orphans who are finally getting a proper education. The school is now ranked number two in the country and is recognized by their nation's president as the leading government school in Tanzania.

We've also built a partnership with Saint Joseph's Hospital in Moshi, Tanzania, and we opened Summit Happy Home, a private orphanage in Arusha, now with our first ten children, fully funded by K2 Adventures Foundation. It is one of the most magical places on earth where we can pretty much do anything we need to ensure that these kids are taken care of at all times. They receive three meals a day, clothes, guidance, and love.

We're adding other destinations. Each time we do, we go into these communities first, let them know we want to do community service, what that would look like for them, and how we can help. People in need are always willing to listen, and once they know what we're about, we embrace the possibilities together.

"This is what we have," they tell us, "and this is what we need."

In Nepal, we've built four small schools throughout the Khumbu Valley for families affected by death on the mountain, and we have also built in Peru, working with the Sonora del Carmen School for the Disabled because it is easy to work there with the Catholic Diocese.

Back home in Arizona, we provide local, adaptable recreational programs, like K2 at the Batcave, K2 Crafts, and K2 Kitchen Adventures.

K2 at the Batcave is amazing. We've partnered with the Colten Cowell Foundation, which owns the actual Batmobile from the original TV show. This is the brainchild and passion of Charles Keller, who bought the Batmobile and built a replica of the cave from what he saw on television, along with a host of other features straight out of Gotham City. He even constructed a life-sized replica of Wayne Manor. Inside this cave is the Batcycle, Batcopter, Batmobile Parachute Pickup Service Van, and of course, the Batmobile. Charles allows kids with a disability or terminal illness to be Batman for a day and ride in the Batmobile, which is one of every kid's dreams, even big kids like me and Kevin.

We met Charles Keller only two years ago, purely by "divine coincidence," and it didn't take long before we were up and running with him, offering all these wonderful programs.

Just as I found such inspiration with Sadie, Charles found his in a little boy named Colten. Through the Make-A-Wish Foundation, Colten's family asked if Colten could have a ride in the Batmobile before he died. When they arrived, Charles threw the keys to Colten's dad. "This is your ride, not mine."

Colten passed away two weeks later.

"This is my destiny," Charles said. "I'm supposed to do more."

One little boy brought a middle-aged man to a place of such empathy and generosity. It reminds us that one moment can change an entire life. Charles now sits on the board for K2 Adventures and we are lucky to have him.

One of these days, I need to get Michelle into the Batcave and see how my champion real-life Batgirlfriend reacts. Michelle and I met ten years ago, just when we were each starting Mother's Grace and K2 Adventures, and we clicked immediately. She eventually came with us to Tanzania and got to see what we were doing internationally, in addition to what we did locally. I think this expanded her view of what Mother's Grace could be, in a spiritual sense, because I see so much of life comes through that lens for her, driven by faith, love, and hope.

Mother's Grace partners with K2 Adventures Foundation for many reasons or occasions. For example, if they need to put a wheelchair lift on the back of a vehicle and we can share the expenses, then we work together through the foundations to give that family a better opportunity. We do this kind of thing all the time and it works perfectly.

Kevin met Jennifer Noelani Spenser and her son, Kainoa, through Michelle. Jenn serves on the Mother's Grace volunteer committee. What she's been through with Kainoa, and how he copes with his severe disability, is an inspiration to all of us. He is kind, funny, and so bright. As soon as Kevin met him, he called me and said, "You need to meet this kid."

Kainoa is a gift who came into our lives for a reason and now he works with us at K2. He has summited Mount Kosciuszko in Australia, and he also works in the Arizona governor's office. This young man has purpose and focuses on helping others. He's also started a nonprofit division of K2 for limb loss. Kainoa chairs a golf tournament every year and works with people who have lost arms and legs to get them adaptive limbs. All in a day's work.

When I go to sleep at night, my heart is full and I sleep quite well. I know that someday, when I die, my family will be able to say, "Look at what my mom did. Look at the path she created, and how can I continue her legacy and be the best person I can be." I love knowing that I've set a good example for my family to grow and help people.

My son, Tyler, met Sadie some years ago. He changed the perception of disability for us. His attitude woke people up to take notice of how kind people can be. Sadie is our north star. We started our organization in 2009 with twenty-six board members, and here we are, ten years later with fifty-plus, and all of them know Sadie's story. This is an honor for Kevin and me because we started as a small organization in my kitchen; now we have an office building and a great team.

Working with individuals who are underserved, especially within the disabled population, is what drives me every day. I simply don't like to see people who do not have a chance to do what they want to do. Whether they're in Arizona, Nepal, Peru, or Tanzania—it doesn't matter. I don't want anyone to tell them they can't do something because they're "different." I tell them we *will* figure out a way to do whatever it is they want, even if it's just once.

Failing isn't what we think it is.

You can't fail if you try; you just can't.

JENN

Tuesday, May 10, 2017, began an odyssey of pain, fear, grief, joy, faith, and love—all mixed together and felt more deeply than I ever imagined a human being could experience.

I was attending the annual Mother's Day brunch for Mother's Grace, which I've been part of for many years, beginning as a volunteer and later as a committee member and company sponsor. My connection with Michelle and the whole group had been such a blessing, a perfect complement to the work I was doing as a philanthropic Realtor who gives away commissions to charities.

Just a couple of days earlier, Kainoa, a sophomore at Seton Hall University in New Jersey, texted me a photo of him at his formal. The school year was almost over, and as a leader of his fraternity and student government, he was busy with that and final exams and packing up to come home for the summer. With a double major and minor totaling eighteen credit hours, Kainoa didn't know anything other than full speed. He loved everything except the crappy New Jersey weather, especially the long winters. No matter how well he prepared, he could never get used to the cold, gray days with no sun, and he felt like his body could never fully adjust.

In spite of that, Kainoa was a healthy, thriving kid, nineteen and doing his thing, with excellent grades and a big bunch of friends.

Sunday morning he called.

"Mom, I'm hung over, and I've got studying to do. I've got to pack, and I'll be home in two days."

He sounded perfectly normal. That night, around 1 AM, while studying in the library, he called again.

"Mom, I don't feel right. It's not like I'm hungover anymore; I think I might be sick."

I figured he was exhausted, and maybe he had a cold or, at worst, a little touch of the flu.

"You just need your mom, Kainoa," I told him, laughing a little. "Just get home."

A reassuring motherly thing to say, as I was concerned, but no alarms went off. I suggested some cold medicine, but when Kainoa called me Monday morning, he sounded alarmed.

"Mom. I just blacked out during my finals. I hit my head on my desk and saw stars."

I called his local doctor to get him a prescription for a strong, three-day antibiotic, just in case, because he would be flying the next day. That night, when Kainoa called, he sounded like he had a bad cold coming. No reason to panic. He texted later to say that he was done packing, but his leg kind of hurt because he had hit it on a box.

The next morning, Kainoa was limping, according to his fraternity brothers. Nothing drastic, but he wasn't walking normally. Later that night, with his plane scheduled to leave early the next morning, he told me that when he went to lie down he felt a sharp, stabbing pain in his leg, and his breathing tightened up. His Apple watch tracked his heart rate at 141, which of course is not right for a kid lying in bed, doing nothing.

By the grace of God, a fraternity brother drove Kainoa to the hospital. Panic set in with the realization that my son was being rushed to a hospital because of chest pain. His leg was hurting badly, but I don't think he mentioned it in the ER before being released two hours later, without a test being done, told to go home, take ibuprofen, some cough syrup, and rest.

I called the hospital to see if they thought he could fly. For some reason, I trusted their word, like we were brought up to do, that Kainoa was okay to fly. I had to trust that somebody was looking out for my baby boy.

He had a low-grade fever, acute, indescribable pain and tightness in his chest—all signs of sepsis protocols, which they did not investigate. The leg pain was never addressed either, and even if he didn't mention it, they never asked Kainoa if he had any pain. At that point, all I wanted was to get my son home.

Just let Mom take care of you.

I called the airline to arrange for a wheelchair to take him to the gate and to pick him up in Phoenix. When he got off the flight, he was wearing a white T-shirt, but he looked even paler and whiter than his shirt. The pain in his leg became worse and he struggled to breathe. My mom and dad were with me, and while Kainoa seemed so sick we were just happy to have him home and out of the hospital. Whatever it was, it was something we could take care of, right?

As soon as we got him home and I saw the inside of my nineteen-year-old's thigh, I had him soak in an Epsom salt bath. He wouldn't stop about the pain in his leg. Everything was happening so quickly. By the time my husband helped him into bed, we decided to get Kainoa to a hospital. Our rescue dog was jumping and wouldn't stop sniffing Kainoa's leg. She must have known that something was wrong.

We reached the emergency room a little over an hour after he landed. Thank God we had gotten that antibiotic in him; otherwise who knows what shape he might have been in? The intake staff was flabbergasted when they saw a fresh hospital band on Kainoa's wrist, dated the same day, from New Jersey. His blood pressure was so high they had to give him Valium to bring down his heart rate before they could give him any heavier meds.

"My leg is on fire."

That's all he kept saying.

After a doctor proposed that Kainoa might be suffering from cramping or dehydration, I jumped in, making it clear that this was no leg cramp. A small bruise had turned into a golf ball and my panic kicked up into another gear. My husband and I wanted CAT scans, an MRI, or whatever they had. Kainoa was being admitted to the ICU. At that point, I still thought everything would be okay, until a nurse put her hand on my shoulder.

"I'm sorry," she said.

"You're sorry? For what?"

"Stop worrying about his leg," she said, "and worry about his heart. It doesn't look good right now at all."

The doctor actually said that an hour and a half after being in the hospital and without doing an EKG. How did they know? By then, the thing on his leg had grown from a golf ball to the size of a baseball. They were still trying to get answers. That's fair; they're not magicians. From what I found out later about necrotizing fasciitis, they waited a long time to do a biopsy and it took just as long for them to figure out that his body was going into septic shock.

The problem with necrotizing fasciitis, like a heart attack, is that there's a window of time to treat it and when it closes, who knows? He should have been flooded with antibiotics in New Jersey because the infection was now spreading unchecked through his bloodstream. His leg grew dark and purple.

"Mama, there are missiles going through my leg; get me help."

It was horrific. We were freaking out in the ICU until they got some serious drugs into him to calm the pain and make him sleepy. I knew that I had to surrender to the medical professionals, that no amount of mothering was going to cure this, but I still did not fully trust what I was seeing in that hospital.

I literally got on my knees and prayed for those physicians and nurses. Right there in corridors of the hospital, on the floor, in the ICU room, in the waiting room, nonstop—I prayed and I texted every prayer warrior I knew on this planet to get on their knees and start praying, too.

"His kidneys are now failing."

This news didn't come as a total surprise, but the doctor said those five words with such precision, they cut right through me. We needed a kidney surgeon right away. A surgeon came in and told us that the necrotizing fasciitis is a flesh-eating virus, which had reached the surface of Kainoa's skin and was blistering through it.

"No one survives this," the doctor said, which marked the second time we had been told that we were losing our son.

"We're very sorry. We are going to go in there and do everything we can, but just letting you know where it's at.... His chances of survival are very slim."

Thankfully, Kainoa was drugged enough by then that he didn't know what was going on. My husband and I, in a matter of five seconds, had just been told that our son would probably not survive the surgery and we had to give our permission for them to amputate from the bellybutton down if necessary.

Go save our son's life.

How can you trust in the Lord under that kind of pressure? I found out that day exactly what it means to do that, when it was literally all I had to go on, as I gave the green light for them to take away the entire lower half of his body, as if I should have the ultimate authority to make that choice.

Was I fooling myself? We surrendered and signed because, by the grace of God, Kainoa survived the surgery and did not lose himself from the belly button down. Instead, they only had to take his left hamstring, from his knee to his buttocks, at least for now, until the next one.

At that point, with a 2 percent chance of recovery, we were desperate to find better options. Mother's Grace became involved and orchestrated a move to the Mayo Clinic in Phoenix, which was better equipped to handle Kainoa's situation. It all began when I called Michelle early in the morning, apologizing for the time, but none of that mattered when I told her what was going on. She immediately reached out to Angela Ducey, our beloved First Lady here in Arizona.

Angela wasted no time contacting Mayo, which saved Kainoa's life, pure and simple.

I knew that God had blessed our journey through Mother's Grace, but I was out of my mind at that point, panicked beyond reason at the thought of losing our son. I surrendered my faith to a higher power because I was convinced that only God could make a miracle happen. I was trusting in the Lord to save my son's heart and soul and body.

Mayo sent an ambulance and put Kainoa in a medically induced coma to keep his heart and lungs functioning. Once again, we signed more papers after they explained that this would keep his internal organs stable, but there was a chance he could lose his extremities because of the extended lack of blood flow. What choice did we have?

We were astonished that doctors from another hospital were rescuing Kainoa because this doesn't normally happen, as different institutions have different protocols and politics, and also because of insurance billing practices. It was all so unprecedented—so many barriers were crossed that day.

We had to sign a financial responsibility contract to go out of network, which committed us to pay Mayo on our own. While we knew this could be the end of us financially, we were committed to doing whatever was necessary to give Kainoa a chance.

Once they got him incubated, we were allowed to see him. No one would look us directly in the eye, as we were the poor parents with the dying young son. Walking down the hallway at Mayo was the longest walk of my life. Then I felt the presence of God upon entering Kainoa's room. This was distinctly more than the white lights of the hospital. His room was simply glowing.

My gosh, God. You've got him. I asked the nurses to keep a Christian station playing 24/7 on the television, as people in a coma can supposedly hear things around them. I knew Kainoa would find comfort in that.

Mayo had a team of nurses and doctors around him nonstop. It took almost forty-eight hours to determine that he had contracted strep A, a one-in-a-trillion chance, from just breathing it in somehow, then bumping his leg, which pocketed the infection, mutated it, and left it dormant in his body. Eventually, it was going to burst, poisoning his body and sending him into septic shock.

They did four surgeries on his legs before they got to the amputations, always thinking they could spare him, but his feet were quickly turning black, and his hands, too, and then his ears, his nose, his penis—all the external parts—everything was turning black.

Okay, that's fine; there's plastic surgery. I just need my son.

Someone showed up with Kainoa's Bible. One of the seventy people in the waiting area, family and friends praying for him, found a four-page handwritten letter inside the book.

"To Papa and Grandma."

I handed it to my dad to read it out loud, another sign from Kainoa that we had a warrior fighting among us who needed all of our prayers.

That's exactly what I wanted right then—prayers for my son, whose given name is Christian: Christian Mason Kainoa Spenser, and he goes by his Hawaiian name, Kainoa, to honor our heritage. That's where the #LIVELIKEKAINOA began, with everyone sharing prayers online via social media.

No matter what the doctors were telling me, I believed something different, and that beautiful letter falling out of the Bible was a sign for me that he would live. By the way, the address of Mayo was 5777

East Mayo, which is such a spiritual number with the triple sevens, meaning you are on the right path serving your divine life purpose.

I was looking for any sign I could find, anything to hold onto, just to keep moving and counter what the doctors were telling me, that Kainoa had two hours to live, and then two hours later he had two more, or four more, but he was never out of the woods. In spite of that, I was not going to give up. Tell me what you're supposed to tell me, and I hear you and respect you, but that's not the only option.

Michelle and Angela came the next day. I had never met Angela. She was a beautiful and graceful soul, and I was so taken aback that she would take time to come see us and bring something, too, a statue of Mary, which she had brought back from Spain, blessed by the Pope!

Michelle gave my husband a rosary from Mother Teresa's home in Calcutta and one from the Vatican, which we kept close to Kainoa.

This was a mother to mother, angels on earth visit from Angela and Michelle. That's just what they do and how they share their hearts in the community. Now it was our turn to reap those blessings. Angela and Michelle kept showing up, bringing me gift cards and salads and comfortable pillows because we slept on chairs in the ICU waiting room for nine solid weeks.

Mother's Day came next, the day of my son's sixteen-hour surgery to have both legs removed. That morning at 5 AM, we heard someone playing a grand piano in the giant atrium of the hospital. The sun was rising, and as we looked down, we saw an old man sitting in his gown, hooked up to an IV, playing "Hallelujah," as if he knew, as if he was setting it up for Kainoa to survive. It was Kainoa's favorite song and a sign from God that our warrior was fighting. We invited that energy and love into our hearts.

I remembered what a doctor had told me on the first day when we arrived, when he put his hands gently on both sides of my head.

"Do you see your feet?" he said.

I nodded.

"That is all you have to look at, and you have to just keep them moving. That is the only thing you have to do, every single day. Just put one foot in front of the other and just keep taking a step. Someday you'll be able to look up at the sunrise, but you can't right now, so just keep putting one foot in front of the other."

I managed to hug every single one of the surgical team that morning as I gave them my blessings and prayed for their hands.

"God is here to guide you, not take you," we said to Kainoa. "We know you're in there and you're fighting. We've got the best doctors taking care of you. Jesus is guiding you, so keep fighting. It's not your time."

One of the doctors pulled me aside and hugged me.

"During pre-op," he said, "Kainoa grabbed my hand and squeezed it a couple times."

I knew he wouldn't make that up. Our boy was showing them. I felt incredible peace. It was Mother's Day, and sixteen hours later a doctor came out to speak to us.

"Can you believe he's here? He made it. I really didn't think I was going to see you again, but he made it."

I told him the story about Kainoa squeezing his colleague's hand.

"Jennifer. You know it's absolutely medically impossible for your son to do that?"

"Okay, Doc. It wasn't me; I didn't claim that. Your renowned surgeon said it."

Kainoa ended up losing one leg above the knee and the other just below the knee. He lost the knuckles on his left hand, which functions now like a paw with a brace, and they were able to save the nub and half of the thumb on his right hand.

He can grab small things with his right hand. That's huge. He can feed himself, brush his teeth, and write. His nub is unbelievable. He does have prosthetic hands, but it took so long to get insurance, and they only gave him eight fingers because they counted the nub as one and his knuckle as another, which is ludicrous, and I'm being polite.

Thanks to the K2 Foundation, we were able to get him his remaining missing fingers.

Those insurance folks brought out the crazy mama bear in me.

"What if it was your son? Would you tell him he only needs eight fingers?"

Kainoa was told he'd never walk again, and a year-and-a-half after being discharged from the hospital—with twenty-four surgeries and skin grafts so far—he *is* walking again.

During the month he was in a medically induced coma, we feared that Kainoa could be brain damaged, but thank God he miraculously regained all his faculties. That said, his last memory from the intake room at the first hospital was totally blurred and he had no idea he was waking up as a quadriplegic. The last thing he knew, he was a college student, feeling sick with a painful bruise in his leg. Now, lying motionless in a hospital bed, he had no idea what had happened and what his future held.

His first words on a letter board were "How's Keanon?," referring to his younger brother. He wasn't worried about himself. The nurses and doctors were close by, in shock, ready to do a brain test when they realized they may not have to, that Kainoa had retained full function.

He had a tube down his throat and was heavily medicated, but he could move his eyes and he knew us. I think he may have woken up a little bit smarter than before.

It took about two and a half weeks before Kainoa could speak, so we communicated through the letter board. He remembers hearing for the first time that he lost his hands through his physical therapist. The black and purple ears and other extremities slowly healed as he came back to life, one miracle at a time.

While we were still in the ICU, he spoke his first words. We walked in one morning, the room was glowing, as it often did, and Kainoa had a huge smile on his face.

"Good morning. Good morning, Holy Spirit."

My husband and I fell to our knees.

"Son, if the Holy Spirit is not alive in you, then I do not know what is."

God and time have been healing Kainoa ever since. It's been grueling, with an endless amount of follow-up care, grafts, therapy for nearly every body part you can imagine, and a long road to rebuild his psychological strength.

The angels of Mother's Grace kept checking on me, asking how they could help.

"You saved my son's life. You got him into Mayo. I don't need anything else. I'm here right now, you're showing up, and I don't need anything else. Thank you."

All they saw was a mom in distress who needed love and support. We were facing a challenge to re-do our house to accommodate Kainoa, and Mother's Grace stepped right in to make that happen. We stayed in one of their guesthouses for three weeks until our house became newly accessible. Then Michelle came over and talked with us about possible options for Kainoa.

"You have to meet this organization, these wonderful people who don't see limitations for people with disabilities. All they see is possibilities. They take people like Kainoa up to the top of Mount Kilimanjaro."

Less than two years after being released, Kevin took Kainoa to the top of Kosciuszko, using a handcycle. I still shudder to think of it and celebrate this triumph every day.

It's incredible to watch how Kainoa has adjusted, defying medical odds. I'm blessed to be his full-time caretaker because as you can imagine, when you've been through an ordeal like this, there are psychological twists and turns along the way. It's best not to be alone during transitions. A song, smell, light flash, or a beep can send him into a panic attack. I am grateful to help him in times like this.

He began sleeping better after weaning himself off opioids in one month, with the help of an opioid reduction specialist and cannabis coach. Now he claims he has Jesus and cannabis by his side. Cannabis is a natural healer. My family, being from Hawaii, knows what it did for my father-in-law when he was doing chemotherapy. We've found that it eases anxiety and stress, and helps with difficulty eating and sleeping.

Kainoa is now working part time with K2 Adventures and interning at Governor Ducey's office. He's back in school at Arizona State University in their Civil Economics of Thought and Leadership program. He hopes to return to Seton Hall, perhaps for grad school.

He's only twenty-two, with a long life ahead of him. K2 Foundation has been instrumental on so many levels. He just launched the first Live Like Kainoa golf tournament to raise money for people with limb loss and limb difference, and to help people get a service dog or other services they need. Kainoa saw what the community did for him and his family, so he wants to give back.

We've been lucky and we are grateful, but many challenges lie ahead as Kainoa gets older and the healing continues. He still has to figure out who he is with his newly defined body and the limitations that come with it.

He recently gave a commencement speech at his old high school on the themes of truth, beauty, and goodness. That's Kainoa in a nutshell, and I'm convinced these qualities will carry him along just fine. There is no doubt his servant heart will shine bright, touching many beautiful souls, as these angels of earth have touched ours.

This experience has enabled me to become better equipped to help others. I am now an advocate at Mayo and Kainoa works there as a medical patient actor in their school of medicine.

I have licked the floors of hell. Now I want to help others. I know about fear and confusion and anger—and how numbing they can be. Becoming a mom of grace has been a journey of turning hard times into holy times, believing in hope during your darkest days, and allowing your weakness to be open to the light of the Holy Spirit and the prayer warriors that surround you!

P.S. FROM MICHELLE

From the first time I met Kristen, I knew she was a powerhouse. I wanted to immediately ditch the sushi joint we were in and hike up Mount Kilimanjaro with my newfound friend. Eventually I did, however, the work we do together is more powerful than hiking. We have joined together now at least ten times to provide assistance to the disabled, and one case stands out, with a mom named Marjorie.

Her eleven-year-old son, Cody, got hit by a bus on his way home from school and was left in a semiconscious state. A year later, his beautiful mother is caring for him all on her own, without transportation to take him back and forth to his rehabilitation center or for any of his numerous medical appointments. He remains in a vegetative state, so Mother's Grace and the K2 Foundation worked together to provide the family with their own medically equipped van, which according to Marjorie, has been life changing.

Kristen and I remain committed to partnering as often as we can. As Jenn knows firsthand, Kristen works wonders for so many families, and I feel lucky to play a role in that.

#What Is Your **GRACE**?

PRAYER

It's funny. When you slow down from the hectic hustle of work, errands, and kids, you can see and hear God *everywhere*.

After my mastectomy, feeling no energy and little confidence, I drove to my son's school for an end-of-year party. Everyone let me know that they were praying for my recovery. I felt the light of God upon me in that moment. When I spent time with my sons that afternoon, I really slowed down to talk to them and, more important, to listen to their feelings. Later that day, I still could not shake the horrible fear and dread of asking myself and God if I would be okay.

On my way to a doctor's appointment, desperate to deal with my anxiety, I was driving slowly (new for me), praying in my mind for peace, and an answer to my needs. As I pulled into the parking lot, it came from God instead. I looked up and saw a sign flashing.

NO ACCESS TO CEMETERY

I knew this sign was a sign to me, and I began to cry, as if God was telling me that I will not have access to the cemetery, certainly not from breast cancer. I walked into the appointment feeling a new confidence, not from me or the doctor, but from God, exactly where it should have originated. God was saying "Stop panicking!" because you will be okay. There will be awful days, with your share of bumps and bruises, but you will not go to the cemetery for this. My prayers had been answered.

What are your prayers?

9

Nikki Haskett:
TAKE ME TO THE RIVER

Bloom where you're planted.

—St. Francis de Sales, Bishop of Geneva

MEET NIKKI HASKETT

For most of his life, my dad was one of the directors for the Department of Interior for the West Coast. He worked closely with Geoff Haskett, Nikki's husband, whom I met when I was ten years old, when he would hang out with our family. My dad and Jeff were two peas in a pod, saving wildlife and the environment through the Bureau of Land Management. As an adult, I followed Jeff on Facebook, especially when he was fundraising for the polar bears, which I loved seeing.

I saw when he and Nikki were married in a beautiful wedding. It was surely a no-brainer when he suggested that Nikki become a part of this book. I always wanted to include a mom working her magic with the environment or among wildlife (thanks, Dad), and it came as no surprise when I felt an immediate divine connection to Nikki, whose wonderful energy just zoomed through the phone line right away.

My former sister-in-law grew up in Grants Pass, Oregon, where Nikki is from, and I've witnessed firsthand what a great community it is and the splendor of the entire physical surroundings, which are God's country, for sure.

Nikki has devoted her life to preserving the treasures of our natural environment and educating people about the value of doing so, especially when it comes to the great riverways in her home state of Oregon. She has maintained her diligent efforts in spite of a life-threatening illness, which nearly took away her ability to speak and communicate effectively. The same will and determination she brought to healing herself and her family has been steadily applied to preserving the beauty and sustainability of our environment.

Here's to my fellow Oregonian and nature lover, Nikki Haskett, in her own words.

I have always been excited about the river. I grew up in Grants Pass, Oregon, a small town in the southern part of the state. I essentially grew up outside, right on the Rogue River, camping and fishing because my parents are both big fishermen, and that's just what we did as a way of life. My dad was a teacher, and in the summer we got in our VW camper and drove around mostly eastern Oregon, camping anywhere we could. My dad told me I could get a college degree in fisheries and I thought that meant I could just keep fishing, which is almost exactly how it turned out. After graduating, I started working for the Forest Service on the Lower Rogue River, checking permits and running the permit system for people wanting to float the designated "Wild and Scenic" portion of the river.

Wow, this is great, I thought, figuring I could keep that job forever. They told me I was a little overqualified with my fisheries degree so I ended up getting hired as a fish biologist for the Bureau of Land Management at the Medford District. I worked in the field, hiking up and down mountains, streams and canyons, doing fish surveys, snorkeling surveys, and salmon spawning surveys. I couldn't believe I was getting paid; I loved the work so much. Many of the fish that we worked with were threatened or endangered under the Endangered Species Act. I learned a lot about the ESA and enjoyed this aspect of my job.

Some of my colleagues didn't care for the whole process, but I produced positive outcomes, which helped my career and got me recognized as someone people could work with on all sides, bringing them together for a common cause—to protect the fish and the river.

My career took off not long after I had my two amazing kids. When my son was three and my daughter had just been born, I found out I had a brain tumor. That was 2003, when I had just turned twenty-nine years old. I had a ten-hour surgery at the University of California, San Francisco (UCSF) Cancer Center, which, according to me, at least, is the best in the whole world. They kept me awake while they mapped out my whole brain so they could focus on the speech area of my brain, as I had an ultra-rare, slow-growing, malignant tumor in my speech center. They weren't sure if I'd be able to speak again, but women are lucky. We have two speech centers, one on the left and one on the right, so if they remove one, there's a good chance that the other would take over, and mine did. By the way, men are not so lucky in this regard, as they only have one speech area. Oh gosh, I know, I've heard all the bad jokes on this subject and I am just incredibly grateful that I survived well enough to tell them in my own voice and to laugh at them, too.

I recently did a presentation in my daughter's class because Madison is a sophomore now in high school and they were studying the brain.

"Mom, can you come in and do your thing?"

It gets them every time.

"How do you think I'm speaking right now," I begin, "because my whole left speech center was removed during brain surgery?"

They kids just look at me like, "What?!"

I went on to explain how I had the surgery and went back home, and then what it was like to have a two-year-old and a nine-month-old baby while also going back to work. I actually couldn't read or write for some time, but the kids helped me recover. I knew that you can get those skills back through forcing yourself to read and write, which recharges the brain, and it did. I read them stories every night. At first, it was very difficult, but they helped me fill in the words. We learned to read together. Within weeks, all my abilities returned. I also had a major seizure, and when I went to the hospital they said, "That's your brain basically reengaging."

Soon after, I worked for four years on a major project, the Western Oregon Plan Revision, which tasked us with looking at new science to harvest timber in a better way to protect local streams. Luckily, after having major brain surgery, I was able to work part time on this very cool project from home for the Oregon State office. I made major presentations to a lot of people and the challenge of having to do that basically rebuilt my brain. I never had any formal speech therapy.

The success of that project prompted them to ask me to work in Washington, DC, where I became the program lead for the Endangered Species program. At the time, it was kind of rare for someone my age to be the program lead. Normally, that's a position for senior-level people about to retire, but because of my experience with the ESA in Oregon, I was tabbed to do it, and I loved every minute of it.

I focused on finding efficient ways to allocate funding for endangered species. That meant working with the U.S. Fish and Wildlife Service and other agencies, along with the Forest Service and Park Service. We pooled our resources and agreed to start the Endangered Species Recovery Fund. Instead of spreading around the existing money to all endangered species, the group worked to target some species that were close to recovery and we worked with state directors to create some easy success stories. We started with a pilot program in Utah and everyone there got on board. Although I'm not with the program any longer, it has recovered more than seventy species, so they are no longer threatened or endangered under the ESA!

This is one of my proudest accomplishments.

From there, I moved into National Conservation Land as a Division Chief and Deputy Assistant Director, in charge of oversight of those lands, which are spectacular and breathtaking. Many of them are designated for the wildlife species they contain. I made trips to the California coast, and one summer my husband and I took our kids camping up the California coast for two weeks. We stopped in the California Coastal National Monument before returning home, remembering all the elephant seals we were able to see on the beach. Every time I visit a unit I'm so thankful that we have these incredible resources available for the public and I realize how fortunate I am to have the job that I do.

I'm not out in the field anymore protecting salmon but what I do in the office, educating people on policies, writing policies, and working on budgets, is equally important. Right now, since my cancer has returned, I need to keep pushing through radiation and chemotherapy, but I come to work every day because it's that important to me.

Nature is in my blood. I grew up on the Rogue River, which was one of the first rivers to be designated as "Wild and Scenic." As a public user myself, a fisherman, I so deeply appreciate this access. In other states, like Texas, there are not many places left to fish at all. There is no public access! So to have these places right in my backyard is a gift, especially when I can share it with my kids and see the joy they have just fishing and hiking and being outside.

My family just went to New Mexico for two weeks and I took them out to Kasha-Katuwe Tent Rocks National Monument. It was amazing to see the looks on their faces when they got there. I can't imagine our country without these places. I don't think they all have to be designated wilderness spots or national monuments or national parks, or even made into great places that are congressionally protected, but it's important to me to have these places to go to because it keeps me healthy and alive and I think our future generations need that, too.

From the minute they were born, I brought my kids out in the river and waded right in with them on my back. Even after my brain surgery, when they were still so young, the river played a big role in my recovery. In fact, if I hadn't had access to those public lands, I wonder if I would have healed as I did *plus* have the chance to expose my kids to this gift of nature.

Six weeks after they cut my head open, we went down to the Coos River, which is not an easy place to access, to go salmon fishing. We walked in the sand in bad weather and I was changing diapers as we fished. Thank God I was able to set this example for my kids. My son is a senior in high school now and he started his own fishing club. My daughter is a teen and still asks to go fishing, and she always catches the biggest fish. She loves the river, too, like me.

In this age of cell phones and computers, it's so important for children to have some balance and a healthy relationship with the earth. I believe our future depends on finding that balance between what we can do indoors and all that is available to us by sharing in the beauty and wonder of wildlife, nature, and the wilderness.

Children need to know these places exist and they must have access to them. This needs to start at an early age so they are not afraid to leave the couch and their electronics and go outside and touch things. My daughter was picking up frogs by the time she could crawl. I think this exposure builds curiosity, appreciation, and resilience. It also means that our future generations will respect the land and all that it offers.

This is why I enjoy the educational aspect of my work because if we don't teach our kids, they may not learn enough on their own. My children, and many others I have exposed to this world, don't throw trash out the window or snicker at the idea of hiking. Sadly, I've seen plenty of kids who have not been exposed to nature who simply have no feel or respect for it at all.

You don't necessarily have to grow up on a river or live in the woods to have an appreciation for public access and recreation for the lands we manage. What's important to me is to make sure that people know what's out there and what's important. A lot of this effort goes toward exposing people to the places I grew up with and love. Not everybody has the same upbringing as I do, that's for sure, but it's never too late to start.

A lot of people are stuck in a place of fear. I've done a lot of research about this, and I think a lot of fear is about safety, for me as well. I used to work alone out in the field and I had a lot of experiences around safety, so I don't necessarily want to go hunting or fishing in certain areas by myself, especially as a female. I've been out with people who live in cities and they get scared and don't want to be left alone. It makes them nervous to be out in the woods, in a remote place, where things are unfamiliar. They watch *CSI* and scary shows on TV. To me, the number-one thing driving this fear is how our culture has changed so that you can't necessarily be out in the wilderness if you're a single woman by yourself without feeling some level of fear, and I don't know how to address that, but it does exist.

There is also a base fear of the unknown that we all have, I guess.

People have aversions to change because they grow up locked into a familiar comfort zone, and they are not too interested in stretching themselves into something new.

The other thing is a lack of education. People just don't know what precautions to take so they stay home and miss out. We're always working to remedy that. Several nonprofit groups have researched how we can reach out best to people of different cultures and life-styles. We often base our approach on a traditional 9-to-5 family schedule. But when we looked at other demographics, we found families with parents working in the evening who were being left out of our programming. This new input made our process more diverse and inclusive, which is a great way of becoming more emotionally intelligent.

My tumor was in remission for eleven years. When it started coming back, I got on a special modified ketogenic diet as part of a study at The Sidney Kimmel Comprehensive Cancer Center at Johns Hopkins in Baltimore, Maryland. I did radiation over a year ago, but that's done. They were supportive at work, so I would just run over to the hospital around 3 PM, get the radiation done, and then work the rest of the day. Besides the brain surgery, it was one of the hardest things I've done. The worst part was the mask I had to wear. It felt like I was being buried alive. The radiation attendees just get you in and out, and they were great, but it was traumatic.

My husband, Geoff, is my biggest supporter. He comes to every single thing I do. I also have the best team of doctors in the country. When it comes to my experience receiving chemo and radiation treatment for a brain tumor, I must say I was most surprised that no one really told us what to expect during that first day of radiation— I mean *really* what to expect.

We drove over there the first day; I had the radiation done, and then—what? Your life is just supposed to continue. I didn't understand why nobody was there to tell me anything about how I was supposed to deal with this radiation protocol, and the fear, and just keep working and taking care of my family. It was all so surreal and bizarre.

I started chemo later. It was delivered like a little Amazon gift to my front door. I did three months of one drug before I had to switch to another, and I'll be done in a few months.

It's been weird because my kids are eighteen and sixteen now, and as teenagers they see the world differently, and that probably includes me, too. They have a new set of fears and less room for mine. That's the natural order of things, I guess. It's their way of protecting themselves. I was surprised at first, until I realized they weren't little kids anymore, and I think they thought I might die, and who wants to confront that?

I try not to even act like anything's wrong around them when they ask me how an appointment went, and sometimes they come with me, but rarely. They've been around this since they were babies, but I've never let it become a part of me or our lives. For the most part, they don't think about feeling bad for me, which is probably the healthiest thing for them.

They're old enough to understand some of the basic science and that people die, that we're not all superheroes. That said, they see me as this strong woman going through all this stuff, as if I'm indestructible. When I told them I was going to have to start radiation, my son had a pretty strong jab of his own.

"Oh my gosh, Mom, did you eat too many doughnuts?"

They say these things, not meaning to be hurtful, but I feel like I must have done something wrong because I'm not this strong person that they see. I'm just me, like one of the salmon in the river, trying to keep swimming.

This brings me back to my childhood. My parents gave me such a gift, empowering me to chase my passion, and I learned to power through obstacles and keep on track with my mission, what I'm so deeply passionate about—wildlife and our environment.

There's a place on the Rogue River called Pierce Riffle County Park. I grew up down the street from there and my brothers and I used to ride our bikes and walk through it all the time. There are green mountains everywhere and you can look down the river really far, coming around a corner, and there it is—a beautiful sky, with fir trees, a perfect scene, so peaceful, and there are no people whenever I go.

I was there again recently on a visit home and walked out to this part of the river. I've been there many times, and it's always so beautiful and peaceful. It's where I go. It's not protected; it's just my spot. It reminds me of a movie, *A River Runs Through It*. I wouldn't describe it as spiritual but this river in Oregon just runs through me and gives me perspective that everything in life is important and beautiful. I would love for everybody to have a spot like that in the future, a comfort zone they can call home.

When I stand there in the river, it reminds me that there's an opportunity for everybody to make a difference. Even when you're going through something difficult, like having your entire speech center taken out, you still matter and you can still affect people in positive ways.

I'm still vertical! I don't think about having a brain tumor. I'm not afraid. I overcame it once and I will do it again. When I start to worry about it, I just don't. I think about something else. I try to stay positive. If I really need to, I go to that trusted place in my mind where I'm in the river, in my place of constant peace.

P.S. FROM MICHELLE

I am in complete admiration of everything Nikki has shared. She told me that she didn't think she fit in with the other moms here, but she does! These women were inspired in their youth, largely by their parents, which is a gift. For me, my dad influenced my appreciation of nature and my mom spurred my interest in medicine and caring for people.

Another thing all these women have in common, Nikki included, is that we make light of our struggles. I've seen this in all of the stories. When Nikki speaks about "running over to get a little chemo," she not only made me laugh (as a fellow cancer survivor), she made me stop and marvel at her humility and how she handled this challenge.

Each of us deals differently with our fears. Some people find a spiritual place to handle it alone, perhaps through meditation, while others find solace and peace with family or through work. Nikki explained how she treats her struggles technically by separating her illness from the rest of her life and not thinking about it when it's not an immediate issue. That's a gift, and Nikki is lucky to have it, no matter where it came from. She's a strong woman who has been through tough times, but being strong is not how we must fully define her, even when she keeps working, gets radiated, does chemo, and still puts dinner on the table for her kids. I think Nikki is much like all of the women in this book. We don't want to be seen as strong women. We want to be *real* women, who can be nurtured and cared for during our struggles.

#What Is Your GRACE?

PEACE

There are so many anecdotes about peace. We commonly hear phrases like, "The only way around it is through it," or "Let go and let God," or "There is a reason for everything," or "Once you accept that life is hard, it isn't hard anymore!"

For me, true peace comes only with an absolute release or surrender into God. As a cradle Catholic, I grew up thinking that God is a powerful man, dressed in white and filled with light. With that in mind, I try not to picture God anymore but just feel His/Her presence. That said, I'm not here to define your "God." But I truly believe in His grace and mercy, and I feel those gifts more easily through prayer. For me, prayer brings peace. It is my form of meditation, and I must make time for it because it's a discipline that offers me balance for intense anxiety. May God give me strength with that.

How do you find peace?

10

WHAT IS *MY GRACE?*

grace

[grác] *noun*

> the exercise of love, kindness, mercy, favor;
> disposition to benefit or serve another

We all come to philanthropy in different ways. Some make an impact through writing checks while others want to get their hands dirty and volunteer for Habitat for Humanity or another group like that who get in the trenches with the people who need it most. Some people need a little push to make a difference while others may react when they're shocked by a human catastrophe. God knows there are plenty of souls in pain who need help right now.

My personal journey through darkness and healing through faith is still a work in progress and this ongoing process has allowed me to pull this book together in a way that could only be divine!

After my second child was born, I had a dream that I should write a book called *A Mother's Prayer*. I was enjoying a spa day, trying to recoup from a difficult birth and a month of no sleep. I fell asleep during a massage and awoke to a vivid dream, telling me to write this book. I was not a writer and had never thought of writing a book—ever! The dream was so compelling that I knew in every cell of my body that it was my divine calling. The fact that it took eighteen years illustrates my lack of faith in myself and my utter fear of being a fraud.

Who the hell did I think I was to write a book?

God kept knocking on my door, over and over, first with the dream, and then the New Orleans trip, the Africa trip, and then my cancer—actualizing what I was trying to write about—along with my son's illness, my career in health care, and the divine meetings with all of the women in this book.

Do I believe that God did these things to me to get me going? No, of course not. I believe all of it was my destiny and that my role in all of this was to make something positive from all of the hardship, a bloom of sorts after the rain.

Writing this book and working with the Mother's Grace organization is healing for me. I know deep in my heart that my mother's prayers are being answered as she now knows that I am finally at peace.

This past Christmas, that peace was put to the test in the form of a prime rib. It was the first time, following my divorce, when my boys' father was not with us. Instead, I invited the man I am dating and his daughters to join the four of us, along with my sisters, cousins, and their children. My boys in college just wanted consistency when they came home—the same bed, same food, old friends, and no hassle—just chill. My sister had been really sick for a few weeks and I didn't have the usual benefit of her creativity preparing the table and holiday aesthetics. I was just happy she could join us in time for dinner. My boyfriend's daughters wanted no part of this "family" Christmas, which I understood because why would they want to hang out with obnoxious potty-mouthed frat boys?

I don't think anyone else was contemplating all of this except me, the mom who wants everything to be perfect for everyone. What mom can't relate to that? I had decided to cook a prime rib for the first time in my life, which was also the same night I was hosting sixteen people for dinner, under the same roof for the first time.

I went to Whole Foods and bought the most expensive piece of meat available. I studied recipes and solicited advice from everyone I could, including my friend, Romy, who became my partner in crime and private beef preparation therapist. I called my dad and even consulted with my hairdresser, who had the perfect closed-door method.

The night before Christmas Eve, I woke up at 3 AM in a panic and started poring through recipes for prime rib. One said I should take the prime rib out of the packaging and let it dry out in the fridge so it will form a "crusty" edge, so I jumped out of bed and ran to the fridge. I actually ran as fast as I could and tore open the packaging. Beef blood flew across the counter and all over the floor, not to mention what it did to my favorite pajamas. After cleaning up, I decided I should take the blood-soaked towels outside to the garbage can. It was pitch dark and I tripped over my son's basketball, dropping everything everywhere and falling straight on my knees, which are now forever scarred because of the prime rib perfection drama.

On Christmas Eve day, I got up a few hours later at the crack of dawn and was first in line at Bed Bath & Beyond when they opened at eight. I found what I thought was the perfect roasting pan and a high-tech, digital meat thermometer that has the receiver on the outside of the oven so you can follow along during the whole operation.

On my way inside, I stopped to talk to a homeless person who needed some Christmas cheer. I didn't have any cash, but I figured I could take care of him on my way out. As I was explaining this, Romy called.

"Hey Hon, I'll catch you on my way out of the store," I said.

He nodded as Romy yelled into my ear.

"Michelle, who is Hon, and did you drag somebody to the store with you at this hour?"

Oh my God, I was I talking to both of them at the same time, trying to help a homeless person while still dissecting the saga of that $250 piece of meat ad nauseum with Romy.

That was absurd and she and I started laughing hysterically. I was inside the store by then, bent over, nearly sobbing with laughter, while holding on to a giant pan and a thermometer that looked like a weapon from *Star Wars*. The idea that I was wasting all this time and energy on a piece of holiday meat while someone needed basic attention did not escape us at all. It was so ridiculous we couldn't stop laughing at how stupid we were.

Back home, I got my frat boys posing as sons to help me understand the instructions for the meat thermometer and in no time we were all yelling at each other, freaking out because it was not working and the prime rib had to go in the oven immediately! Finally, my middle son mastered the thermometer and we put the giant piece of meat in the oven. All I had to do is cook it for one hour (alarm was set) and then turn off the oven and let it cook (closed door) for three more hours. That was it. If I just did that I would produce a beautiful prime rib, and just to make sure, I had the handy-dandy meat thermometer keeping track of it all.

I checked the oven every five minutes to make sure I didn't miss turning off the oven at exactly the one-hour mark. My sister called and I got involved with her for about twenty minutes, trying to make her feel better and letting her know how much I was hoping she would come. That's when I realized I had not showered and people would be arriving in less than an hour.

Inside the shower with shampoo in my hair, jamming to Christmas tunes, I suddenly screamed at the top of my lungs.

"Oh my God, the prime rib!"

I had let it overcook. I ran to the kitchen and checked the thermometer, which read *done*. We would be eating way sooner than I was ready for so I took the roasting pan out of the oven as I didn't want it to cook for one more second. I started slicing the hell out of that prime rib and then stopped to call my brother-in-law for advice.

"Take it outside," he said, "and let it cool down first."

I put an aluminum foil tent over that giant piece of meat and walked back inside. Within a minute, it was pouring rain and the prime rib was getting soaked. I hustled to protect it. That poor slab of beef had been through a lot in twenty-four hours, not to mention my nerves. Keeping it tented saved it from getting waterlogged. I stuck it back in the oven long enough to reheat it but not cook it any more. It was a little dry, but not bad, and we all had a good laugh about my exploits.

Are you a mom who is always trying to make things perfect? Well, don't! Life is messy. It's tough and bloody, and it gets rained on sometimes. Something as stupid as a prime rib can become a metaphor for life—bloody, messy, troublesome, and only as hard as you make it. But, just by letting go, a journey unfolds and yellow flowers continue to bloom.

Have you ever looked outside the window of an airplane and watched the hamster wheel of activity down below? You see people that look like ants, scurrying from one square acre block to the next, buzzing through a maze of traffic and obstacles. Whenever I travel for work, which seems to be more and more often these days, I settle into my window seat and stare outside as we take off and land, wondering what everyone is up to, and why all of their activity looks so small and mundane and even pointless, like hamsters urgently going nowhere.

As we reach our cruising altitude and I take time to reflect, I realize that many of the people I observe from 30,000 feet are actually connected to each other, that they are not just a bunch of little dots bebopping from one corner of the earth to the other, for no reason at all. They are bound together intimately by common fears and hopes, faith and dreams. They are us, and we exist in this world for one another!

We need to remember that and honor it.

You don't need to start an organization to accomplish grace. All that's needed to begin is curiosity, a generous spirit, and a willingness (and maybe a neon vest for visibility) to expose a bit of your heart and soul to others who need more than just tangible support. They need to be seen and heard and recognized as full and flawed human beings, just trying to survive whatever trauma they or one of their family members is experiencing. When we encounter these people, we must slow down and do the right thing, which is often quite simple. We can even take the liberty of seeking out connections to people who are fundamentally just like us, yearning to find deeper meaning in our lives and to make a difference in someone else's.

I've spent most of my life feeling the absence of my mother, but I've never gone a single day without feeling the tingling sensation of her love, or hearing her whisper in my ear to make sure to do something meaningful with my life. If only she could see my three growing boys becoming remarkable young men. If only she could see the face of my oncologist, first delivering the news of my diagnosis, and years later, delivering news of my cure. If only she could see the monthly board meetings of Mother's Grace when these powerhouses come together to make their next plan for moving mountains and saving lives.

I recently hosted a happy hour and my friend Delcia said something special to me. "Your mom would be so proud of you."

That was the nicest thing anyone ever said to me. I really believe she is with me daily, in spirit, as I continue to expand my efforts to ease the burden of as many women as I can. We do this through the coordinated effort of organizations you've been introduced to in this book, as well as with new individuals and groups we are meeting every day. It's my mission to help launch their endeavors by equipping them with the tools to start their own nonprofit organization, with their own unique agenda and creativity.

Supporting these phenomenal women is surely making my mom proud, and I can think of no better intention in life. I know what I want to keep doing. Now it's *your* turn to figure that out for yourself and get busy. When you gaze outside the window of any plane going anywhere, there will always be someone in need, fearful, in pain, and feeling lost, yearning to make a meaningful connection. You can become a part of that in so many ways. The possibilities are infinite. Take that one step forward, lay down your fear, make a call, and tell a friend to just show up.

HOW TO
CREATE YOUR OWN
PHILANTHROPIC MISSION

I've been absolutely terrified
every moment of my life—
and I have never let it keep me
from doing a single thing I wanted to do.

—Georgia O'Keeffe

I t's clear for me that my grace is found in praying the rosary to Mary, the mother of our Lord, and finding my own path through meditation, love, and peace. If you are inspired to walk in the footsteps of the many moms in this book who have founded charities that are changing the world, or better yet, would like to get involved with an established charity that needs your special skills, let me offer you a brief, high-level beginners' guide on how to get started.

This also serves as a reminder of why this book exists in the first place—to pay it forward with love and grace, mother to mother, mother to family, to heal the world.

I hope this book has given you the opportunity to take a fresh look at the challenges in your life and how you can choose to rise to whatever occasion is calling you. I am asking you to define your calling to do more interpersonal work, to be present, pay attention, get off the phone, and look around. Elevate your family life at home, give back to your community, and take a chance and do something to support one mom, twenty, or even an entire community.

Mother Teresa said it best: "Not all of us can do great things. But we can do small things with great love."

This begins by exploring what inspires you, opening up possibilities for discovering new positive outcomes, and altering the trajectory of your own life story. It requires honest self-assessment and a hunger to increase our resilience so we are best equipped for our journey, which will be rocky at times, full of doubts, and laden with obstacles.

We can look to Tracy Cockerham for an example of someone who has made this happen. After losing her twenty-year-old son, Connor, also known as "The Ginger," in January 2014 to melanoma, Tracy made it her mission to eradicate this life-threatening disease. In Connor's honor, she co-founded IMPACT Melanoma, which, along with the Melanoma Coalition, have joined forces to fund research for a cure and to support education and legislative reform.

Tracy provides an inspiring example of a mother turning her rarified grief into a concrete and active passion for helping others struggling through a similar ordeal. She proves my theory that moms who have experienced overwhelming life circumstances are the best ones to reach out to communities and share their hard-core stories.

Lee Rhodes, while in the midst of her third battle with cancer, turned the serenity of making original art into her life mission—to create an exceptionally beautiful product while providing resources to help others. She founded glassybaby, which makes handblown works of art, such as glass candleholders. A portion of each sale of these unique pieces is donated to the White Light Fund, which has given more than $10 million to nonprofit organizations that provide hope and healing for families in need.

When I was going through cancer treatment, a dear friend gave me a glassybaby and I've had it on my nightstand ever since. Ten years later, Mother's Grace was the recipient of a grant from glassybaby, another result of a serendipitous, divinely inspired meeting.

During my time with cancer, those who had walked my path before me became the people I sought out for advice. Ironically, and in true grace, my stepmom became my mother. As a seventeen-year survivor, no one was more supportive or able to understand my struggle.

Expert coping advice, like psychologist Angela Duckworth offers in her book, *Grit: The Power of Passion and Perseverance*, might also help many of us trying to figure out the best and most effective way to pay it forward.

> There are no shortcuts to excellence. Developing real expertise, fig-
> uring out really hard problems, it all takes time–longer than most people
> imagine. And then, you know, you've got to apply those skills and pro-
> duce goods and services that are valuable to people. Rome wasn't built
> in a day. And here's the really important thing. Grit is about working
> on something you care about so much that you're willing to stay loyal to
> it. It's doing what you love, but not just falling in love–staying in love.

This type of passion is what binds all the mothers in this book.

THE SIX BRANCHES TO GRACE

All it takes to begin is taking one step forward, inspired by a dream or a yearning to do something. You may want to start your own 501(c)(3) or volunteer at a local hospital, holding drug-addicted babies. You may want to write a book or start a social media campaign. Whatever it may be, all that's holding you back is fear.

But fear does not need to render you motionless. Here's what you can do, one step at a time, according to what I call the Six Branches to Grace. I firmly believe you need to be in touch with God and the world, and most of all your true self, before you can fully realize your own divine journey. Take a stab at the following suggestions that got me started.

1. Grab a notebook.

I believe our phones may be our demise, distracting us from the beauty of the world. God does not come to us on our phones. God's grace comes in the connections we make with our family, friends, pets, communities, and co-workers, and to those desperately in need of a hand to hold during difficult times. So put your device down, look up and around you, and start to tune in to God's signs and guidance.

Just like Sister Mary does everywhere she goes in India, take a notebook with you and keep articles and assorted things inside it that move you and feel important. Write like a banshee every time something pops into your head. I carried around a red leather notebook for eighteen years. I filled it with articles, advice, photos of inspiring scenes, ideas, quotes, and small pieces of what became content in this book. Make that notebook your own personal project, like a vision board coming to life.

2. Pray.

Pray to your God, the universe, or a higher power. To me, prayer is meditation, a release into God's grace. It's a total letting go to what will be, and when I have no distractions, I can feel a buzz throughout my body, like every cell is alive but calm. Just find a routine that works for you. I don't believe there is a right or wrong way to pray, but closing your eyes and asking for God's presence can change the trajectory of your day. There is an amazing podcast that has assisted me in this process, called, "The Shocking Secret You Must Know to Create Lasting Behavior Change with John Assaraf."

3. **Listen to inspirational music.**

I have my own "innercise" and exercise playlists and after listening my blood is pumping, primarily from great music that gets my ass in gear and makes me appreciate how precious life is.

My favorites include

"My Wish," by Rascal Flatts
"Don't Blink," by Kenny Chesney
"Live Like You Were Dying," by Tim McGraw
"Yellow," by Coldplay
"Yellow Ledbetter," by Pearl Jam
"Right Now," by Van Halen

It's amazing how music can get you going. My friend makes me the most amazing playlists and whenever I am mad or down I listen to them. This reminds me of how he feels about me, and any petty stuff I may be feeling just melts away.

Now it's your turn to make your own inspired playlist.

4. **Read!**

I've always been a reader. When I was five years old, I joined a book club in the summer and if I read ten books, I got a free book from the library. I was thrilled to get that new book—the smell, its feel, and the sense of a new adventure. When you're seeking a quieter, more internal form of inspiration and comfort, *read*! Keep three or four books by your bedside with a highlighter and read for an hour before you go to sleep. I struggle with this one because at night I like to "check out" mindlessly on Netflix. That means I must force myself to slow down and read, and I'm never sorry when I make that choice.

Here are some of my favorites:

The Power of Now, by Eckhart Tolle. Life changing for me on the actualization of how to become present.

Mother Angelica's Little Book of Life Lessons and Everyday Spirituality, by Raymond Arroyo. Talk about a kick-ass nun. *OMG*! She teaches how to "live your life like a prayer." If you can take this one thing from the book, this is it!

A Return to Love: Reflections on the Principles of "A Course in Miracles," by Marianne Williamson. I reread this ten times and still grow every time I open it.

The Shack, by William P. Young. No cheating: read the book before you see the movie. It's a beautiful, phenomenal story of pure grace.

Grit: The Power of Passion and Perseverance, by Angela Duckworth. I make everyone who works for me read this book. It's pragmatic and intelligent.

The Road Less Traveled, by M. Scott Peck. I was thirty when I read his quote: "Once you accept that life is hard it isn't hard anymore." This idea remains profound for me.

The Lorax, by Dr. Seuss. One of my favorite childhood books that I still find meaningful. It's about balance and the importance of doing the right thing when it comes to preserving the natural world.

How about just reading the Bible? All the wisdom you need is right there. Psalms is my favorite section and if you need a daily pick-me-up just read Psalm 23:

> THE LORD IS MY SHEPHERD; I SHALL NOT WANT.
> HE MAKETH ME TO LIE DOWN IN GREEN PASTURES:
> HE LEADETH ME BESIDE THE STILL WATERS.
> HE RESTORETH MY SOUL: HE LEADETH ME IN THE PATHS
> OF RIGHTEOUSNESS FOR HIS NAME'S SAKE.

Okay, moms, what's better than that? Doesn't that sound better than the spa? Green pastures? Still waters? I realize it's a metaphor but come on. . . .

5. **Enlist your posse.**

This is of upmost importance. If you don't have one, create one now. Put together a group of girlfriends who have your back, who you can talk to in the upmost confidence, and who will tell you like it is—lovingly at first, but they should also be willing to hit you over the head, if and when you are being ridiculous. (Confession: I have bruises all over my head.) As you develop your ideas, ask for their opinions and steady feedback. They should also hold you accountable and keep you moving. I called on my posse throughout the entire process of writing this book and developing the charity.

Over the last ten years, I've formed a writing group, a travel group, a birthday group, a lunch group, and a prayer group. These special women have carried me through more than any one person in my life, and they are way cheaper than the $150 to $200 bucks you pay for 47.5 minutes with a therapist. (Yes, I like therapists, too, but the older I get the more I appreciate the strong women in my life—my posse.) You can start with one "bestie" and grow it. No games, no agenda, no drama—just pure friendship.

6. **Secure a project partner.**

This may be key for you. I could not get all of my ideas on paper, which made my situation seem insurmountable. Had I not found my project partner, it would have taken me another eighteen years and I would be in an old folks' home, still trying to write this book. Tell people your goals. Be honest; lay your fears aside and tell the people you have recruited that they will become like vehicles to help you find the right people. You may have to pay your project partner, but that is why they are experts in their field and worth your investment. Aren't you and your goals worth it, too?

Project partners can be writers, life coaches, therapists, trainers, spiritual advisors, and/or editors, but whomever you choose, it should be someone who can hold you accountable. Paying for these services holds me way more accountable to the process and keeps me motivated and on track. If you can't find the right fit for your philanthropic mission and you genuinely feel like your idea fills a gap in the world, then you can start your own 501(c)(3).

HOW TO START A 501(C)(3)

Before I started Mother's Grace in 2009, I had no idea what a 501(c)(3) was or what it could do. I knew that all kinds of charities existed, but I had no idea how they were started or how they operated. When I decided to start a charity of my own, I staged a garage sale at my house, raised some money, and then gave it to someone who needed it. There was no paperwork or administrative records; it was a single act of goodwill, which is enough to get anyone started. If you just decide that you can change the trajectory of someone's day, week, month, or year, and you take a first step to make it happen, then you're on your way. It *is* that simple.

I chose to make a difference.

When I saw what $500 worth of gift cards did for a family with a child dying of a brain tumor, I was all in. I wanted to do more and more. I went online and Googled "how to start a charity." One link led me to another, and I reached out to a certified public accountant (CPA) and got the application for a 501(c)(3). I also recommend going to the site *councilofnonprofits.org*, which lists valuable information to help you.

Here are the next steps.

Step 1: Jump!

Take one step toward what you want to do. Make one call. Research one topic. Sit in on one meeting of a charity that you like. One step is all you need to begin.

Step 2: Start the Paperwork

Look at the paperwork online here:

www.irs.gov/charities-non-profits/application-for-recognition-of-exemption

Read through it in pieces. If you feel overwhelmed or if you are somewhat ADD, like me, you may have trouble concentrating on the forms. In that case, look up a local CPA who handles the formation of nonprofits. Fees vary, but doing the paperwork yourself costs anywhere from $250 to $700 and you can find many good tutorials online.

If you feel like you're 50 percent ready to go and struggling to get over the finish line, contact a local CPA. Their prices vary, like any other service provider, but depending on what state you live in, you can find a good one for anywhere between $300 to $3,000, depending on how much help you need.

Finally, if you don't want to do any of this yourself or simply don't have the time, you can hire an attorney who specializes in this work. He or she will cost you anywhere from $2,000 to $10,000, depending on the nature of the 501(c)(3), how quickly you'd like it done, and your particular state's regulations. I did a lot of the work myself before hiring a CPA who helped me refine my answers. Although she was the most noteworthy CPA in Arizona who specialized in nonprofits, it cost me less than $1,000.

Step 3: Form a Board

Once you get your paperwork completed declaring your organization's status as an official 501(c)(3), it's time to recruit people for your board of directors, if you haven't already. I began with only three board members and over time we grew to thirteen individuals. The trick is to find people you trust who embrace your mission for all the right reasons.

Here are four types of people I suggest:

1. Someone who brings advice and guidance in areas where you are not strong. For example, my first board member was a former attorney who *loved* going deep into the details. That's not my thing. I'm a big picture gal, and this woman saved my ass more times than I can count and kept us growing in the right way. Thank you, Leanne!

2. Someone who shares your vision and who can speak passionately about the mission.

3. Someone with expertise in law, finance, business development, and/or program development.

4. Someone who is a "doer," who is willing to roll up her sleeves and get things done because when you first get started you can't pay a staff so you need board members who will work for free—volunteer—and not complain.

Step 4: Create Bylaws

You can find standard bylaws all over the Internet, which are fairly boilerplate, and you can add your own specifics. For example, you can decide how many meetings members must attend, or how much they must donate to the cause, both financially and through time spent. Start at a high level and let it evolve over time. I always like to include confidentiality agreements and have them re-signed each year. (Again, available as boilerplate on the Internet.)

Step 5: Business Development

Business development is made up of five to six specific pillars. If you put together a strategic road map for each of these pillars and just keep adding to it, you have a starting place.

- Marketing
- Project management
- Networking
- Fundraising, raising capital
- Operations

Marketing can be as simple as a website and a brochure on what you want to do. To paraphrase that old advertising adage: "Tell them what you're doing, do it, then tell them what you did." Your marketing can be as simple as that.

Project management is where your board or committee comes in. Find the right people to do the right things and empower them to own it and push forward. For example, in a 501(c)(3) you can have someone in charge of researching the project plan, someone in charge of talking about it, and someone to execute the plan.

Networking requires finding a person who is passionate about your mission. Most of the time that should be *you* because you know the story and the vision. Talk about it until you are blue in the face; get people excited; tell them success stories; get them involved; and pretty soon they'll tell the story for you. I have many examples of this, but now I have someone 3,000 miles away, talking about Mother's Grace with a passion, and she's got droves of women ready to start Mother's Grace East Coast. It all started in a Starbucks, sharing my passion with like-minded moms.

Step 6: Social Media Marketing and Branding

I'm no expert in this field and I'm not crazy about it at all, but creating a brand and promoting it through social media is a necessary component to get your message out there. If you're not a pro, then hire your teenage daughter, who will rock it for you. Seriously, there are thousands of pros out there that love this stuff. Start with a visual that tells your story and a message.

Our visual hook is the fleur-de-lis, which means many things to many people. The stylized lily was a symbol for royalty; it is a symbol for New Orleans and the Saints football team; it's pretty jewelry; but to me and my gals, it means the Holy Trinity and Mother Mary. She is the ultimate symbol for motherhood. We added leaves to represent a mother in bloom, supporting others and lifting them up. Find your symbol and make it meaningful to you and your message; then spread that all over town—and all over your website and social media.

Stick to your guns if you have a vision. Listen to feedback from trusted others, but you know best. I have pushed back on many who have tried to change my concept, but I went back to the drawing board until finally after twenty renditions it clicks and is just so right.

Step 7: Fundraising

There are many types of fundraising options, but you may want to start small.

- CrowdRise is a great app to get things going (but watch out for fees). Explain your mission. Put it out on social media. Ask your friends and family to send the information to their contact lists. Rinse and repeat. Then do it over and over with a *new* message. My friend Romy just did this with her mission (Wight Horse) and raised $10,000 to get started. That's a lot more than my piddly $2,000 from a two-day, hot and sweaty garage sale.

- Host a lunch at your home and tell everyone about your mission, leave pledge cards on their seats, and humbly request their consideration for contributions to get you started.

- Partner with a restaurant, yogurt shop, local business to donate a portion of the proceeds of a weekend sale. Promise them you'll blast social media about their business in return.

- It's amazing how many retailers do these programs and are happy to host your organization. Our first year, we went door to door to ask for support, and just because it's 2020 it doesn't mean old-fashioned cold calling will not work. Try it and use the 1/10 rule: make ten calls and get one positive response, which will energize you for days. I know because I did it.

- Once you get your feet wet, you can start asking for sponsors. There are plenty out there with charitable dollars to spend. I'd say that 90 percent of businesses do some type of charitable giving. After ten years, we now have people calling *us* offering to give us money.

- Seek local, regional, and national grants, and private donations. If you can't afford to hire a grant-writer, contact your state arts organization for help.
- Go to lunch with your local community foundation representatives. They're trained to hold donor-advised funds. The more you are in front of them, the more they will "understand your mission," and look for a good fit.

One last thought from Angela Duckworth, as she so eloquently states in *Grit: The Power of Passion and Perseverance*:

> Whatever your age, it's never too early or late to begin cultivating a sense of purpose. I have three recommendations, each borrowed from one of the purpose researchers.... David Yeager recommends *reflecting on how the work you're already doing can make a positive contribution to society.* Amy Wrzesniewski recommends *thinking about how, in small but meaningful ways, you can change your current work to enhance its connection to your core values.* Bill Damon recommends *finding inspiration in a purposeful role model.*

For more information on starting your own nonprofit, please visit the resource link at *www.mothers-grace.org.*

MOTHER'S GRACE
DEO GRATIAS

MORE ABOUT THE MOMS

The world is more
malleable than you think,
and it's waiting for you to
hammer it into shape.

—Bono

As you know by now, each of the women in this book are a force to be reckoned with, a sterling example of resilience, and a beautiful, shining example of turning extreme loss and heartache into something positive, generous, and spiritually healthy. They are brimming with passion and I've seen it become contagious in multiple projects they have launched, as they've recruited highly talented professionals and volunteers to assist in their endeavors.

Once upon a time, these normal moms encountered huge, life-altering trauma and tragedy, which tested their faith and ability to cope. Through some type of divine happening, they started a movement in their living rooms and kitchens, with next to nothing for money and support, and slowly but surely, or in some cases almost overnight, the seeds of their commitment grew into something much greater than themselves, as they have all plowed forward on a mission to make the world a better place, one woman at a time.

If any of them can do it, so can you.

Lori Alhadeff

Make Our Schools Safe

makeourschoolssafe.org

Contact: 609-335-8226

E-mail: info@makeourschoolssafe.org

Twitter: @lorialhadeff and @MakeSchoolSafe8

Facebook: @MakeOurSchoolsSafe17

Instagram: @lorialhadeff8 and @makeourschoolssafe

TikTok: @Lori_Alhadeff_

> *Thank you to Alyssa for being my guiding light.*
> *I miss you so much and love you forever.*
> *Thank you to my husband, Dr. Ilan Alhadeff, for being my rock.*

Lori and her family

Bonnie Carroll

Tragedy Assistance Program for Survivors (TAPS)

taps.org

E-mail: *bonnie@taps.org*

Contact: 202-588-TAPS (8277) (main number)

1-800-959-TAPS (8277) (TAPS helpline)

The Tragedy Assistance Program for Survivors (TAPS) is the national organization offering compassionate care for all those grieving the death of a military loved one. TAPS provides peer-based emotional support, grief and trauma resources, grief seminars for adults, Good Grief Camps for children, case work assistance, connections to community-based care, and a 24/7 resource and information helpline for all who have been affected by a military death. Services are provided free of charge.

Caring for the families of America's Fallen Heroes since 1994.

Bonnie and Drew Barrymore

Bridget Costello

For the Love of Conor
www.fortheloveofconor.com
Contact: 480-217-1806 and 480-217-8556
E-mail: bridget@emeraldconsulting1.com

My Irish grandmother, Delia, shared with me that the one thing you can be sure of is life will offer you agony and ecstasy. As mothers we experience the defeats and successes of our children and our family in a profound way that touches the very core of our hearts. It is important for mothers, especially, to practice self-care because moms are the glue and inspiration of the family. So, don't go down! My family makes a conscious decision to choose joy every day despite our loss and tragedy. I urge all mothers, even in the face of extreme adversity, to stay in a place of gratitude and joy. This is *your* life journey.

Thank you, my dear son, Conor, and thank you, dear family, for choosing joy every day.

Fight like hell though the tough times and enjoy
the hell out of the good times.
—The Costello family motto

Bridget and Conor

Marianne Gouveia

EricsHouse
www.ericshouse.org
E-mail: *marianne@ericshouse.org*

EricsHouse Inc., founded in 2017, provides integrative grief care to people who have lost a loved one to suicide or substance abuse. We support the emotional, physical, and spiritual healing for those living in the aftermath of these devastating losses. Our team of grief specialists, counselors, life coaches, spiritual directors, intuitive healers, and holistic health practitioners help people navigate their grief so that they may move beyond their loss. I thank all of the people we support, especially the moms who have lost a child, for being so vulnerable as to share their journeys and to allow our team to help them heal. And although I would do anything to have my son back, I thank God for giving me twenty-seven years with a sweet boy who continues to teach me about love even through his death. I thank God for carrying me through this crisis with His Grace and Love, and for calling me to turn my pain to good.

We are changed forever, we will never stop missing
our loved ones, but we can carry on with acceptance, peace, and
joy, and we can lift one another up with abundant love.

Marianne   *Eric*

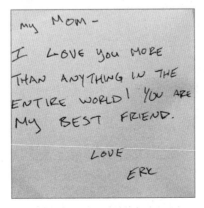

MY MOM —
I LOVE YOU MORE
THAN ANYTHING IN THE
ENTIRE WORLD! YOU ARE
MY BEST FRIEND.

LOVE

ERIC

Nikki Haskett

Organizations I support:

**Sidney Kimmel Comprehensive Cancer Center/
  John Hopkins Medicine** *(hopkinsmedicine.org)*
Southern Oregon Fly Fishers, Inc. *(soff.org)*

I am a working mom with two incredible children, and because of my husband, three amazing stepdaughters and seven wonderful grandkids. I have had the great fortune to have had awesome jobs in the conservation world. I take great pride in my roles as a mother, biologist, and conservationist.

Always put relationships first and be objective. Pursue your dreams and what you love. Love your children. Love your family. Make a difference in the world. Always work hard and do good. Thank you to my husband, Geoff, and my parents, Nick and Jeanie, for always being there for me.

*Eventually, all things merge into one,
and a river runs through it.*
—Norman Maclean, *A River Runs Through It*

Nikki and her kids

Sister Mary

Contact Mother's Grace for more information.

Michelle and Angela in India at the orphanage with Sister Mary

Debbie Moak

notMYkid

notmykid.org

notMYkid is a 501(c)(3) nonprofit organization, founded in 2000, that provides children and families with truly lifesaving programs, support, resources, and education. Our mission for the past two decades has been to empower and educate youth, families, and communities with the knowledge and courage to identify and prevent negative youth behavior. Our impact is far reaching. To date, we have served more than two million individuals and aim to reach 75,000 annually through our statewide and national programs.

> *To whom much is given,*
> *much is required*
> —Luke 12:48

Debbie and Steve

Jennifer Noelani Spenser

Live Like Kainoa
k2adventures.org/k2-golf
E-mail: jkspenser@cox.net

Blessed wife and mother to Kapo, Kainoa, and Keanu. Our *ohana* (family) is extremely passionate about giving back to our community and this has made our darkest days possible to survive. We look forward to supporting our incredible faithful warrior with his dream to help others with the LLK Foundation, which will be in place within a couple of years. Kainoa's mission is to live beyond his circumstances and give back to people living with limb loss, limb difference, and mental health issues, both seen and unseen. I simply cannot express the gratitude in our hearts for Mother's Grace, K2 foundations, and our prayer warriors around the world. We are forever grateful.

> *Ahuwale ka po'okela I kau hana ia ha'i.*
> *It is through the way you serve others that*
> *your greatness will be felt.*
> —Hawaiian proverb

Jennifer and Kainoa with Michelle and Angela Ducey

Kristen Salcito Sandquist

K2 Adventures Foundation and K2 Adventures Travel
k2adventures.org and k2adventuretravel.com
E-mail: Kristen@k2adventures.org

Our two companies combine working with able-bodied and disabled individuals by providing opportunities to become a better version of themselves. We provide an adventure that will check an item off their bucket list and immerse them into the local culture by giving back to the local communities we serve in the United States, Tanzania, Peru, and Nepal. Thank you to Kevin Cherilla for introducing me to international service in addition to the work I was doing in the United States.

The worst thing you can tell someone is that they can't do something that they have always wanted to do.

Figure out a way to make it happen. Where others see limitations, we only see possibilities.

Changing Lives One Adventure at a Time

Kristen and Kevin with two of their favorite boys

Lorraine Tallman

Amanda Hope Rainbow Angels
Amandahope.org
E-mail: hello@amandahope.org

I truly love being a mom. It took almost thirteen years and a lot of prayers for my three miracle daughters. I learned that life is very complicated, but I never lost hope and I never give up. Every day is a gift and I'm grateful.

Big hugs to Amanda Hope and my precious husband, Marty. You taught me how deep love is and heaven-eternity is real. We are called to make a difference, even if it's only a smile to someone who is hurting.

Amanda and Marty

Where I'm weak,
God is strong.
Whenever I'm in need,
I find someone to help.
The circle of Love,
it works every time.

Connie Uddo

Director, NOLA Tree Project
Contact: 504-415-8434
Connie@NOLATreeProject.org

The mission of NOLA Tree Project is growing stronger, healthier communities through tree plantings, community service, and disaster relief programs. The most positive way to combat climate change is to plant trees. Planting a trillion trees would cancel out the last decade of carbon dioxide emissions.

Special thanks to my husband, Mark, for his unconditional love and support of my work. You are my rock!

> *People, even more than things,*
> *have to be restored, renewed, revived,*
> *reclaimed, and redeemed;*
> *never throw out anyone.*
> —Audrey Hepburn

Connie

Romy Wightman

Wight Horse
wighthorse.org
Contact: 602-809-8505
E-mail: info@wighthorse.org

Wight Horse is a 501(c)(3) dedicated to helping the insured, working class manage medical debt. We do this through setting up realistic payment plans and negotiating existing debt to a lower cost, or eliminating debt altogether. Our goal is to provide peace of mind, so families can concentrate on what's important—health and healing.

I want to thank my kids for their laughter and their love.

We only know what today brings.
We have no idea what tomorrow holds,
so live in the moment because our final chapter is a total mystery.

Romy

ABOUT THE AUTHOR

MICHELLE MOORE is a strategic business veteran and a senior vice president for S&P 500's Laboratory Corporation of America. She has received several prestigious awards, including Outstanding Business Woman of 2019 (*Phoenix Business Journal*), First Place in MASK (Mothers Making a Difference), The Hon Kachina Award (Arizona), recognizing the achievement of outstanding volunteers while increasing public awareness about volunteerism, and a Governor's Commendation from the First Lady of Arizona, Angela Ducey, for her "extraordinary service" to the people of Arizona.

Michelle resides in Scottsdale, Arizona, with her three boys and their dog, Rudy. She loves to hike the beautiful trails of her state, listen to great music, travel the world, and connect with mothers from every walk of life.

ABOUT MOTHER'S GRACE

In 2008, I was diagnosed with an aggressive form of breast cancer. As I fought this painful and frightening disease, another major crisis emerged when I had to rush my son to the hospital, where he was diagnosed with Type 1 juvenile diabetes. I became quite isolated while I tried to cope with these dual challenges. I soon felt a powerful need to experience the support of other mothers, directly and without judgment. As a result, I founded Mother's Grace, a nonprofit that now assists mothers and their children in the midst of tragic life events.

Our organization addresses the acute needs of mothers by helping them with housing costs, medication, meals, housekeeping, childcare, transportation, and a host of other immediate needs. We also work one-on-one with mothers to provide emotional support and mentorship to enable them to accomplish long-term success with their own personal missions.

Through professional guidance and seed grants, Mother's Grace also advises women who wish to start their own nonprofit organization. To date, our 100 percent volunteer-driven staff has raised more than $5 million for women and their families in need, and has assisted more than 3,000 mothers in the state of Arizona, and many more throughout the world.

Mother's Grace
Founder/President Michelle M. Moore
480-320-9466
www.mothers-grace.org
Scottsdale, AZ 85254

A portion of the proceeds from sales of this book will be donated to Mother's Grace and organizations led by grace-filled moms who fit our collective mission.